Shared visions emerge from personal visions. This is how they derive their energy and how they foster commitment....This is why genuine caring about a shared vision is rooted in personal visions. This simple truth is lost on many leaders, who decide that their organizations must develop a vision by tomorrow!

Organizations intent on building shared visions continually encourage members to develop their personal visions. If people don't have their own vision, all they can do is "sign up" for someone else's. The result is compliance, never commitment. On the other hand, people with a strong sense of personal direction can join together to create a powerful synergy toward what I/we truly want.

—Peter M. Senge, from *The Fifth Discipline*

From THE FIFTH DISCIPLINE by Peter M. Senge. Copyright ©1990 by Peter M. Senge. Used by permission of Doubleday, a division of Random House, Inc.

Advance Praise for

LESSONS FROM THE WINDOW SEAT

"Finally, a business book that stresses the need for organizations to clearly define their values, but also recognizes that each person possesses differing 'core values.' Mr. Specht's prose style creates a remarkable look at diversity in value perception—a must read for all 'value-centered' organizations."

TOM HILL
SENIOR ASSOCIATE, THE KEN BLANCHARD COMPANIES
CO-AUTHOR OF THE LEADERSHIP BRIDGE

"Perfect for the organization faced with the issue of improving colleague retention. David Specht delivers a practical user-friendly model which helps colleagues see results of their work in the organization through the looking glass of their personal values and beliefs."

KELLY BENNAN
CHIEF LEARNING OFFICER, SEDGWICK CLAIMS MANAGEMENT SERVICES, INC.

"Lessons from the Window Seat lures the reader into one's own relationship with purpose. The vibrant importance of that then radiates toward relationship with others and with the organization. The integration of the individual and organizational purpose as the foundation for vision and mission of the collective provides powerful life energy that fuels a new definition of success!"

VIRGINIA DUNCAN
PRESIDENT, WISCONSIN LEADERSHIP INSTITUTE

LESSONS FROM THE
WINDOW SEAT

ACHIEVING SHARED VISION IN THE WORKPLACE

DAVID SPECHT

Telos
PUBLICATIONS

Huntington Beach, California

PUBLISHED BY TELOS PUBLICATIONS
a division of Temperament Research Institute
P.O. Box 4457, Huntington Beach, California 92605-4457
714.841.0041 or 800.700.4874 / fax 714.841.0312
www.telospublications.com / www.tri-network.com

ORDERING INFORMATION

Individual Sales U.S.: This publication can be purchased directly from Telos Publications at the address above.

Individual Sales International: This publication can be purchased directly from Telos Publications at the address above.

Quantity Sales: Special discounts are available on quantity purchases by corporations, associations, and others. For details contact Telos Publications at the address above.

Orders for College Textbook/Course Adoption Use: Please contact Telos Publications at the address above.

Order by U.S./International Trade Bookstores and Wholesalers: Please contact Telos Publications at the address above.

Cover/Book Design by Kristoffer R. Kiler

The Self-Discovery Process is a trademark of Temperament Research Institute, Huntington Beach, California.
Contract for Shared Vision and Design are registered trademarks of Triumphant Leadership Solutions, Inc.
MBTI and Myers-Briggs Type Indicator are registered trademarks of Consulting Psychologists Press, Inc., Palo Alto, California.

Library of Congress Cataloging-in-Publication Data
Specht, David.
      Lessons from the window seat: achieving shared vision in the
      workplace / David Specht. — Huntington Beach, California:
      Telos Publications, 2000.
              p.   ill. cm.
      Includes bibliographical references.
      ISBN 0-9664624-8-3
      1. Organizational behavior. 2. Work environment. I. Title.
HD58.7 .S64   2000   99-64657
302.35   dc—21   CIP

03 02 01 00 • 5 4 3 2 1

Printed in the United States of America

May 2000

To Suzanne and Donald Specht

Contents

CONTENTS

Foreword

WHEN DAVID SPECHT CAME TO ME WITH THIS BOOK AND asked permission to include our material, I was delighted to say yes. He not only captured the essence of how to use the models I shared with him, but he applied them to many other powerful frameworks. David shows how to create a simple process that readers can understand and apply. *Lessons from the Window Seat* brings an important message that impacts every level in an organization, reaching far beyond the world of business, with applications to every aspect of life.

Lessons from the Window Seat has the power of a teaching tale. The story holds interest and makes learning seamless. As the characters come to life, they animate many popular ideas — learning organizations, Kaizen, value-centered leadership, strategic visioning, self-directed teams — all woven into a practical tool that changes lives.

David has brought a much-needed "how-to" to one of the most long-lived psychological frameworks — Keirsey's Temperament Theory. In the 1970s, David Keirsey began to teach counselors and educators about the four temperament patterns. He had been fitting together the many descriptions of four basic personality patterns since the early 1950s. He found commonalities in the writings of many great thinkers as far back as 2500 years ago. As one of his students, I learned his theory addressed basic psychological needs, values, and motivations. They apply to people both when they function well and when they are under stress. His self-published book, *Please Understand Me*, sold well over a million copies with no marketing or advertising. Clearly, this was a theory whose time had come. Over the years, many people have told me Keirsey's work has salvaged their marriage, saved their child from failure, or helped them run their business more effectively. All of this merely from understanding how people are different.

When I founded the Temperament Research Institute in 1988, I sought to develop and refine Keirsey's powerful contribution. My colleagues and I focused on the essential descriptors of each of the four temperament patterns. We soon realized that once people identify their own core values and needs, they enjoy the possibility of opening up new vistas for themselves. They can be more self-aware and thus take more responsibility for their own growth and development.

David Specht saw the key link between having an individual know his or her own values and the organization knowing its values, then provided a way to integrate them. We are indeed fortunate to have these *Lessons from the Window Seat* to use as a guide to applying this valuable tool.

This book has been needed for a long time.

Linda V. Berens, Director
Temperament Research Institute
author, *Understanding Yourself and Others,
An Introduction to Temperament*

Why Should You Read This Book?

YOU'LL WANT TO READ THIS BOOK WHEN (1) YOU'VE discovered that work is encompassing entirely too much of your life and too much of your identity is riding on success or failure at work; or (2) you're struggling with how to lead others into becoming productive and included members of your team. Since most of us spend the majority of our waking hours at work, dissatisfaction there is emotionally draining and unproductive. Yet productivity is what work is about, and our bosses or shareholders reinforce those objectives, if by no other means than their simple presence.

So productivity must occur, and fulfillment in our working lives is optional. Or is it? At this point in the conversation, most people I work with give me the classic response: "Well it depends."

So I ask them this simple question: when you come home from work, how many minutes does it take for you to bring a work-related problem into a conversation? Unless the kids have been extremely unruly that day, I find it's generally within 10 minutes. Single people take about the same time to start talking about work, though it may be hours before they actually speak to anyone on the phone or in person. Then I ask a second question: does your work affect your relationships at home? In all cases, the answer is yes.

After answering the two questions, I find people quickly seek to justify why they work where they do. They pull out responses that rationalize the importance of their work in altruistic terms. "I'm doing it so I can provide more for my family," or "We're creating technology that will make a difference to our children," are representative examples of what I hear. To these I respond, "Well then, why are you complaining about work instead of bragging about it?"

Inevitably, I listen as more defense mechanisms show their faces until I hear the *coup de grace*: "I have to work; I have bills to pay."

To tolerate your job simply for the pay is to deny yourself the basic joy of living for those hours you spend working. Moreover, those feelings of dissatisfaction from work spill into your "quality time" at home. This book is about turning work into quality time. Having quality time at home is rewarding because we can freely express and satisfy the components of who we are. Our working environment should be no different.

OUR APPROACH

Companies grow. People grow. Companies that fail to grow go out of business. People who fail to grow or, more commonly, grow away from the company's culture and direction, are passed over or let go. Many simply leave. It's not surprising that human resource publications often cite the number one reason for people leaving a job is "to pursue advancement." A euphemism for personal growth? In many ways, I think so.

The trick, then, is to provide a corporate infrastructure that allows for individual growth within the system of corporate growth. More specifically, the working unit (team) must endorse the individual's personal growth while incorporating that growth into the team's agenda for productivity and advancement. Two popular business concepts today identify elements of this belief. (1) "Kaizen" emphasizes promoting the growth of the team by embracing the ideas of its members. (2) "Learning Organizations" plan on improving the productivity of the team by improving the quality of its members — *Learning to Plan and Planning to Learn*, as one popular book is titled.

For those of us in the trenches, the question becomes how to apply these theoretical concepts to our company. We know we have to change because the books tell us about so many logical benefits. We also see our competitors committing to change. "But where to start? How do I know what's appropriate for our unique company? I'm busy enough," are the most common responses I hear.

You will find the "how" in this book. Identifying the needs and values of the individual, and contrasting those with the needs and values of the group, provide a clear picture of "who's in" and "who's out."

The "who's in" crowd, when allowed to prevail, is destined to make many decisions from a *group think* perspective. In other words, since their values prevail, their perspective will be the one used in decision-making. In such situations, those opinions from outside the *group think majority* are usually disregarded as "different" or "not getting it," since they come from a singular or minority point of view.

Group think, while quick and efficient, doesn't allow for differences and discourages discussion. Most people "already know" what the boss or subordinates will say, so they don't even bring up an issue. "The boss and I just have a personality difference on the matter" is a typical statement I hear. In a group think environment, we tolerate the relationships and situations that cause us personal consternation — in the interest of being more productive. Toleration, therefore, is the culprit of our dissatisfaction. Toleration stems from the division of "who's in" and "who's out."

This book provides a process that bridges the gap between the "in" folks and the "out" folks. It then allows you to tap into personality diversity to solve your most pressing problems by using both majority and minority points of view. This process not only reduces blind spots in seeing solutions, but also builds "buy in" from both insiders and outsiders.

THE FORMAT

I've written this book in the form of a fable because I find business theory difficult to translate from the pages of textbooks to the relationships and situations specific to my work. Yet, I often find I'm able to apply the relevant parts of a friend's story about a work experience to my own place of work.

A second reason is to deal tactfully with the obstruction of personal pride. It's quite easy for me to pass judgment on a character's poor decision within the story. In contrast, it's a more bitter pill to swallow when a "self-help book" asks me directly if I exhibit an inappropriate behavior on a regular basis. A story doesn't say anything about me specifically, yet it allows me to see myself in, or learn from, the behavior of the characters.

Finally, I found I have learned as much or more from the poor bosses I have had as from the very best ones. Stories allow us to see what bad and good leaders do without having to suffer through their learning curve as their subordinates. I notice people in real life often make vows to "never do it like he did it." They might not know how they would get the job done, but they do know how *not* to do it. Stories increase our arsenal of experiences without requiring our direct involvement. They serve as friendly analogies of what does and doesn't work, without casting judgment on our own abilities or the abilities of others. For instance, you couldn't give your boss a book titled *How to Lead Your Employees*, but you could give him or her *Lessons from the Window Seat*.

ON READING THIS BOOK

You may be tempted to skip directly to the "How To Get Started" section, which takes you through the process of bridging the gap between yourself and your group. People who do so quickly identify the surface-level needs and values they admire, rather than their true long-term values. Though values "of the moment" are easy to identify, they won't help you with long-term fulfillment. So I highly encourage you to read the story first.

While the story is a fable, it does present the "why" behind the "how." It gives you an opportunity to examine your own feelings about work-related issues on a more strategic basis, rather than simply identifying the issues that perplex you this week. Most people find they can finish this book in only one or two sittings, so read the story. I think you'll find the characters entertaining and the process powerful.

David J. Specht, President
Triumphant Leadership Solutions, Inc.

Acknowledgments

T HE IMAGINATIVE PRESENTATIONS OF THE CONCEPTS IN THIS book were greatly facilitated by Steve Linhart. His many late nights spent editing brought the characters to life, and helped create the allegory needed to teach otherwise difficult theory. Steve's eye for humor in life prohibited me from allowing dull characters into the tale. He insisted the characters represent a variety of values and talents, and that each situation be a skillful representation of real life experience. I certainly wouldn't have been able to jazz up the story as Steve did quite easily from his Artisan perspective.

In addition to Steve, Linda Berens, Ph.D., selflessly gave of her time, her expertise, and in some cases her own material, to complete this effort. The challenge of achieving a shared vision and teamwork without an understanding of psychological need and motivation is simply not possible. Dr. Berens' work in developing The Self-Discovery Process™ has made "being different" both tolerable and understandable, for those of us tired of being pigeonholed by a trainer or counselor into some classification. Her process of arriving at true core needs is a critical component in taking the guesswork out of understanding human motivation. It allows us to move on to shared vision in our relationships. Competence and mastery are core needs to people in the Rational temperament like Dr. Berens. What's unusual is her desire to make a career of sharing her masterful knowledge of personality diversity.

Nancy Schwede, Ed.D., conceived the concept of this book. She shed light on how to translate the principles taught from my training courses into a story format. Without her vision of how this book could be meaningful to others — a unique insight of the Idealist temperament — I would not have moved forward.

As a member of the Guardian temperament, I would never consciously exclude anyone who helped keep this project on the road to completion. My interaction with them was as meaningful as the completion of this book. They made it fun and interesting. The colleagues and friends who contributed to this work and deserve special recognition are (in alphabetical order): John Farese; Natalie Johnson, MBA; Susan Johnston; Michelle Kenimer; Kris Kiler; Michael Knapp; Jan Martin, MBA; Barbara McNichol; April Milne; Kathy Ogg; Brian Luke Seaward, Ph.D.; Lisa Specht; and Christine Testolini.

PART (I)

WHEN
VALUES
COLLIDE

CHAPTER 1

Plausible Personality
Differences

T HE KIDS WERE FINALLY IN BED AND, KNOCK ON WOOD, asleep. Jessica had hit the sack early, but Bob needed to unwind. It was 10:30 p.m., and no one could touch him. This was his recuperation time. The couch was his kingdom. His loyal subject Ben, the family dog, slept at his feet. The paper and the remote were at his command. Bob looked forward to some quiet time each night, but tonight it was even more welcome.

It had been one of those disastrous days at work. Every phone call, every meeting, every email, seemed to bring more bad news. Bob felt shell-shocked by the end of the day, questioning not only the length of his employment, but also why he worked so hard.

At Chip Tronix, Bob was one of five project managers in the Research and Development group. That was — until today's conference call when the president announced budget cuts, taking out four of the five ongoing R & D projects. Bob was now the manager of the only remaining project. His new computer chip became the future of Chip Tronix in one fell swoop. It had been a difficult day.

Bob unconsciously flicked on the television while he shuffled through the newspaper that Jessica had scattered over the coffee table. "Where is the front page?" he wondered. A *Real Life* magazine fell on the floor as Bob lifted the paper. Bob always got a kick out of the "how to catch your ideal mate" type of articles, so he opted for the magazine over the paper.

The magazine floated open to a mailer separating the pages. Sure enough, there it was: "How to Match Your Personality with Your Significant Other." Bob searched for the quiz that inevitably told America's broken hearts more about their relationships. This article didn't have a quiz, though, just some charts. What was this?

Find yourself, then ask your significant other to do the same. Do you complement each other?

IDEALIST

Want to be authentic, and empathic.

Search for identity, meaning and significance.

Relationship oriented, romantic, idealistic, wanting to make the world a better place.

Look to the future.

Focus on developing potential, fostering and facilitating growth.

Generally enthusiastic and inspiring.

Think in terms of integration and similarities, and look for universals.

GUARDIAN

Want to fit in, to have membership.

Hunger for responsibility, accountability and order.

Tend to be generous, to serve and to do their duty.

Look to the past and tradition.

Trust contracts and authority.

Want security and stability.

Generally serious and concerned.

Skilled at providing order.

RATIONAL

Want knowledge and to be competent, to achieve.

Seek to understand principles and theories.

Want to have a rationale for everything.

Future oriented.

Trust logic and reason.

Skeptical and analytical.

Hunger for precision, especially in thought and language.

Skilled at long-range planning, inventing, designing and defining.

Generally serious and focused.

ARTISAN

Want the freedom to choose: be spontaneous.

Want to be bold and impressive, to have impact.

Generally excited and optimistic.

Absorbed in the action of the moment.

Oriented toward the present.

Seek adventures and experiences.

Trust impulses, luck and their ability to solve any problem.

Ability to notice and describe detail.

Frequently drawn to trouble shooting and performing in any context.

Adapted with permission from Linda V. Berens, *Understanding Yourself and Others, An Introduction to Temperament* (Telos Publications, CA, 1998).

Bob had seen personality classifications before. In every team-building session he'd attended, a trainer had tried to shove him into one category or another. Surprisingly, this article said that only the individual could determine his or her personality's "true" temperament. He read the print under the charts:

Only by oneself can a person be honest enough to discover what his or her true values and needs are. During this process of self-discovery, a person inevitably learns some values are shared with others while other values are unique. Moreover, a person needs to look from several different vantage points to see his or her true core needs.

Personality tests, which only overtly test our desired or surface level values from a single criterion, don't allow us to see our deep-seated core needs. Such testing often leads facilitators to the wrong conclusion and the misclassification of the person's temperament. They ultimately confuse us more than they aid us to achieve our fundamental motivations.

Bob was impressed with the author's honesty about the subjectivity of today's personality tests. Bob reread the explanations of the four temperaments. He liked how each focused on strengths, and how each had a specific, unique point of view. But it was beyond him why the author suggested linking men and women of the same type. Why couldn't people of different types be as happy together as those having the same type? Wasn't it possible to share specific characteristics and values without conflict? Why classify everyone in the first place?

Bob's favorite late night show's theme song rang out from the television, and he quickly became entrenched in the political satire of the day. His question about why differing personalities couldn't create harmony faded with each passing joke. The television won out and the magazine drifted back to the coffee table. Bob's recuperation phase had begun.

CHAPTER **2**

Day-to-Day Compatibility

MAN, WHAT A GREAT DAY, HE SAID TO HIMSELF. CLEAN, crisp air, bright sunshine, no wind, and no lift lines to boot. The skiing was so peaceful and the mountain so beautiful. "Where are Jessica and the kids? Oh, they'll be just fine," he wouldn't let himself worry. "I'm sure I'll catch up to them on the slopes," he rationalized. Before he knew it, he was off the lift and back on his favorite run. How did he get on the run so fast? He barely remembered getting off the lift but, no matter, an empty run was an empty run — he was off.

"Dad!" Emma was yelling. "Daaad!"

Where was she? He could hear her so clearly, but she was nowhere in sight.

"Dad, how about waffles today?"

"Waffles on a ski slope? That's odd," he muttered. Then reality set in. He squeezed his eyes shut to postpone the inevitable. He threw a backhand across Jessica's side of the bed. Swat, swat, he missed. The other side of the bed was empty — again. Where was Jessica? Wasn't it her turn to feed the kids? She seemed to always escape on her morning run just minutes before the children awoke.

He bravely opened his eyes.

"Hi Daddy," Emma said. "Can we have waffles this morning?"

"Sure darling," he said, squinting up at her from his pillow. "Can you get your school clothes on while Daddy gets breakfast?"

"Yes, Daddy."

"And wake up your brother please, thank you."

Waffles, how many times had we had waffles this week? It was Tuesday. What did we have yesterday? Did it matter? All that mattered was getting the children fed and off to school in some semblance of order.

It seemed like the morning duty always fell on his shoulders. Jessica had to get her run in before venturing off to work. Getting up early to exercise was something he gave up shortly after high school, but Jessica not only loved it, she always came back with more energy than before she left. He never could understand how she stayed so energized, but he loved her for it.

Her running, though, didn't help his immediate situation. Wouldn't it be nice to hit the shower first and wake up in warm comfort? Boy, those were the days, he thought as he shuffled down the hall to the kitchen. Yes, those single days of long ago were a hazy memory. Taking care of others was his way of life now.

He briefly cleaned the family room on his way to the kitchen. He organized the previous evening's mess and gathered up a stack of newspapers for the recycling bin. The *Real Life* article landed on top of the newspaper pile. Bob stopped cleaning for a minute to re-examine the article. He chuckled to himself as he picked it up. "Let's see . . . do they have a temperament for taking care of others, making waffles, picking up toys, providing a stable environment so others can go for their run?" he asked rhetorically. Bob scanned the four boxes filled with different values. "Tend to be generous, to serve and to do their duty, want security and stability, skilled at providing order." The words from the Guardian section jumped out at Bob. He was shocked by their relevance. He tore out the page, folded it neatly, and stuck it in the pocket of his sweat suit. "This might be fun to review on the plane," he mumbled, thinking of the long flight to Des Moines he'd take later that day.

Bob proceeded to the kitchen to resume his duties. He pulled the frozen waffles from the freezer while his thoughts wandered from waffles back to Jessica. She was doing so well in her new job as marketing director of the women's clinic. Each night she brought home another success story. Whether she talked about new referrals from key physicians or about patients she helped in the lobby, she always made an impact on whomever she came in contact with. And everyone loved her!

"How did she get everyone to love her?" Bob wondered. "To conduct a career in sales where you're dependent on the work of others for your efforts to be meaningful, where a million things could go wrong, how can you still have everyone love you?" He knew she simply made everyone feel important.

Curiosity got the better of him and he pulled out the neatly folded article from his pocket. "Hmmm. Artisans: want freedom to choose the next act; to have and to act on impulses. Want to be graceful, bold and impressive, to have impact!" Well, there she was: Artisan. He read the other definitions, now more interested than ever. But before he could finish, guilt forced him to put the article back in his pocket. What was he thinking? How could he classify his wife, of all people?

"Waffles up!" he announced to the house.

Emma arrived at the table, eager, dressed, and ready to eat. "Thank you, Daddy," she said.

Bob gave her the "once over" inspection. Everything matched and her hair was brushed — check. What a saint. She was in third grade, loved school, and never had a problem in the world. When would this wonderful behavior end? It couldn't last forever, could it?

"Where's Michael?" he asked.

She shrugged her shoulders in response.

"MICHAEL," Bob sent out a homing beacon.

Michael arrived with a shirt, underpants, and no pants, socks, or shoes. "Mike, buddy, you know you can't go to school dressed like this!" Bob stated. "Go back to your room and finish dressing. What do you say?" He grabbed Mike's shoulders and turned around his half-asleep body. "I know this clothes thing is a bum deal, but unfortunately you've got to play the cards dealt to you."

Michael was in second grade but lived like a college frat brother. He couldn't find cleanliness and punctuality on any of his pull-down menu options. In fact, he questioned the importance of anything except playing in the yard and conducting video game battles. But he was a loving kid. All he had to do was pose a question in a cute way, and Bob was at his service. "And why not?" Bob posed. If he could raise this kid to be something, what a success Bob's life would be. Michael was already a ton of fun. His children's temperaments wouldn't be on the chart, or would they? Bob wondered when children developed their personalities. Michael's was already pretty consistent, as was Emma's. Could it be possible they already showed the essential characteristics of personality at such young ages?

"Bob, I'm back," came Jessica's greeting from the back door. Upon entering the kitchen, she assumed command. "Waffles again? Bob, we had waffles yesterday! Well, I guess it's time to go to the store again. Where's Michael? Emma's ready to go. Where's your son?"

"How was the run?" Bob interjected, trying to slow Jessica down a bit.

"Fine." Jessica tuned in to Bob's easygoing pace. "I guess I'm a bit rushed. Too much to do and too much on my mind. What time did you say you're leaving? Sorry to ask again." She threw in the apology out of habit.

"Nine A.M., to Chicago, and then on to Des Moines, then back Friday at 6 P.M., International Airways both ways." He raised his eyebrows while turning to check on his son's progress.

Keeping track of dates, times, and items of rule and order were optional for Jessica in her personal life. Spontaneity ruled the day. To be bound by a schedule somehow reduced the amount of time she'd have to really do the things she felt needed to be done at the moment. Even after ten years of marriage, Bob hadn't learned her exact criteria for scheduling life's important events. They had tried the calendar on the fridge . . . he had given her a personal organizer . . . he would leave notes. It didn't really matter. She always tried to squeeze too much into too little a day, which made her (and him) constantly late for everything. It's a wonder how she got so much done.

"What's this meeting at corporate about?" Jessica asked, sarcastically spitting out the word corporate.

"We're re-evaluating the direction of the new technology. The big layoff they announced has got the remaining people worried. Our project was the only one of five to survive the cut."

"Yeah, yeah, so why a three-day meeting?" she quipped in disgust. Her perception of corporate's incompetence was only outdone by her disdain of its intrusion into her life. She didn't want her husband gone for three days.

"Well, since I'm the project manager and corporate has a large percentage of its dollars in only a very few eggs . . ."

". . . they want to interrogate the hens sitting on the eggs." She finished his sentence for him.

"Right. Except this time they want to discuss overall corporate direction as well," he added.

His answer seemed to quench her curiosity for the time being. Besides, she now had to contend with the clock.

"I'm in the shower. I'll be ready on time this time, I promise," she yelled with a big smile while jogging to the bedroom.

She doubted if corporate could really solve anything in a three-day trip, although she did know he loved his job. He was known as a terrific leader at his office. He cared so much about everyone. For him, what the team created together had more importance than anything he would do on his own. If she headed that office, she would have to know she was uniquely important to what was going on — that she was making a difference. But he didn't seem to need that. Yes, he used his MBA skills and knew the semiconductor business as well as anyone. The last R & D team Bob led designed a multimillion-dollar chip set for a cellular phone company. He just didn't share her need to be acknowledged as a unique contributor. The success of his design group was what really mattered to him. She didn't understand how anyone could be such a "Mother Teresa" in the Silicon Valley, but here she was married to him.

Bob's happiness at work was becoming increasingly important to Jessica. The growing instability at Chip Tronix had caused him, and Jessica in turn, much extra stress. Marrying Bob, however, was the best decision she'd ever made. Every time she overstepped her bounds or overextended herself, there he stood. Always loving her as much as the day they met. Flowers once a month, date night, it didn't seem to matter that two kids

13

pulled them in a hundred different directions. He still made her feel she was the most important person on the planet. He wasn't without faults, of course, like his stubborn insistence the entire family get together on all major holidays — her family one year, his the next. Or insisting the kids do their homework between six and eight o'clock every night. Then there was that time they couldn't go on that free ski trip she had won through work because he had committed to attend a financial planning seminar. Too much order could be a bad thing! "Oh well," she sighed. She loved him and needed him. She needed all of them.

Yet as much as she needed them, Jessica wondered how the four very different people who made up her family could civilly coexist. She was always on the go. Bob was Mr. Orderly. Emma was going to save the world. Michael was a thinker and analyzer. She and Bob took great pride in allowing input from the entire family whenever making decisions. That probably had a lot to do with their success. There was no doubt Bob and Jessica were the parents and in charge, but the four of them were in this family together. They would allow each other to succeed or fail as individuals backed by a supportive group. She wasn't sure how they had gotten to this point as a family, but they had. It was a good place to be.

CHAPTER **3**

Our Challenge: Balancing Work and Life

THE MORNING ROUTINE SWITCHED TO THE TRANSPORTATION phase, made "easier" by the recent addition of the family mini-van. Bob had hung on to his 300ZX as long as possible to conserve funds for more pressing family matters. But life's necessities had finally overtaken him and, as guardian of the family, he made the move to the mini-van. After piling kids, backpacks, and luggage into the van, he actually felt a bit proud of how much "stuff" he could now ferry around town. He started the van and left the driver's door open for Jessica. She always insisted on driving when they were late. Jessica hopped in and abruptly backed out of the driveway.

After several blocks, they approached the school drop-off

area. Flight paths in and out of the international airport seemed to be more orderly. Speed and efficiency were critical as the kids simultaneously unbuckled and headed out the door. Emma kissed both her parents on her way out, and wished her Dad a safe trip. Michael was already out the door. Bob yelled good-bye to him and actually received a wave in return, albeit one that was running away without a glance back. Jessica took a long look at her children, then headed for the freeway.

The drive to San Francisco International was forty-five minutes barring any unforeseen difficulties. Bob's scheduling of Jessica's morning run, school drop-off, then trip to the airport, was on course but provided no room for his usual one-hour cushion at the airport. He claimed he no longer lived the structured life of his Air Force days. Sometimes the virtues of his previous life surfaced no matter how much denial he buried them under.

Jessica actually enjoyed the challenge of the commute. For her, it had become a game and the rules of the game constantly changed. Traffic rules weren't absolute, just recommended, a view which Bob didn't share. As a result, Bob learned to bite his tongue and Jessica learned to use the turn signal, which made driving tolerable for both.

Once on the highway, Bob's thoughts drifted as he reflected on yesterday's conference call to the staff in Chicago. The budget cuts had forced a re-evaluation of all company expenditures. Naturally, everyone in the meeting began pulling out his or her "empire-building" safety nets. He relived the entire intolerable scene in his mind. VPs, Directors and even Project Managers instinctively drew on their tools of survival: be aggressive, ensure budget and corporate structure align with your program; don't justify the arguments of the weak players by conversing with them; fall back on your longevity and importance to the company's bottom line. Everyone knew the projects considered "indispensable" would be saved. The others, and the people who worked on them, let go. Bob had been trying to enter the fray of the conference call to say something positive about R & D when Jessica's voice came on the line. She wanted the budget to include Kleenex.

"What?" Bob responded, questioning Jessica's rude interruption of his conference call. His mind returned to the car and the present.

"Can you please get me a tissue out of the glove box?" Jessica repeated. "Are you OK? You haven't said a word for the last ten miles."

Bob composed himself as he searched for the tissue. "Yeah, I was just thinking about yesterday's conference call on the budget cuts. Seems like wherever I work, there's this vicious cycle in product development. We invent a product, sell it, and have plenty of money for awhile. So we hire all of these folks to build and support the product. During that time, people gladly tell you what they do, how they contribute, and how they envision the company's direction. Yet everyone has a different version. You get the feeling they each work for a different company."

"Vastly varying versions of vision," Jessica blurted out and laughed.

"Yea, thanks Jessica," Bob recouped his thoughts. "Of

course, they're all being forced to build their résumé, or 'empire,' continually. That way, if the company lets them go, or they see a better job elsewhere, they are ready to jump ship. Very few people really talk and help each other. Most people work like crazy on their own project and help others when they have spare time — which, of course, is rarely to never. People concentrate on their own values and stray from the company's values. Naturally, that assumes the organization took the time to define its values and objectives in the first place. That's a big assumption. Companies that don't define their values seem to enter a vicious cycle. It doesn't matter if they are growing or downsizing, they all go through this cycle."

Bob pulled out his trusty personal organizer. Sometimes it was easier to figure things out when they were written down. This might be one of those times. Bob flipped past the neatly arranged addresses and calendars to a blank note pad in the back. He quickly diagrammed his thoughts.

VICIOUS CYCLE

Infusion of
MONEY

GROWTH
Build Infrastructure
Product Development
Support Development

CUT BACK
Streamline Processes
Reorganize Structure
Cut Costs/Outsource

Lack of
MONEY

"We generally start the cycle with lots of money because of a product's success or an infusion of venture capital. We build an infrastructure to support our product and develop others. Before too long, our product isn't so special anymore and we've invested most of our cash in 'growth opportunities.' All of a sudden, we're out of money and have this huge infrastructure to support. The solution, then, is to cut way back and bet everything again on one or two new products. Hopefully, we come up with a second winner, and so on and so on. The cycle may complete itself only once or any number of times. But eventually little companies go out of business, merge, or sell out, and big companies reorganize, cut groups, or combine divisions. Few companies break the vicious cycle and grow long term.

"So why, at the beginning of the vicious cycle when we have money, can't we communicate and coordinate well enough to get to a common vision? After all, we ultimately are forced to reach a common solution anyway to get to the end of the cycle."

Jessica had heard this all before from Bob, but now decided to tackle it head on. "Sounds to me like you guys really do have a vision problem. The same thing happens to us. We'll get a few new contracts, then hire new clinicians and staff. But when some of the referrals we counted on never show up, we've hired too many. We panic, lose some of our employees for one reason or another, and look for ways to cut costs. Ask anyone what needs to be done and you'll always get a different answer. Once again, too many different versions and not a common vision."

Bob considered her response. "OK, maybe you're right. Obviously a company has to have a vision and a mission." He used his hands to show a target high in the air. "At business school, we learned a mission is what must be done and a vision is how things could best be. You've got to do the mission first, or you'll quickly go out of business. Mission is simply 'who, what, and how.' Who do we serve? What do we do? How do we do it? Come to think of it, we only seem to consider the organization's Who, What, and How at the very beginning or the very end of the vicious cycle. Either when we're lined up in front of the venture capitalists to start a company or when we're rearranging an ailing budget to save a company."

Jessica smiled to encourage Bob to continue. She usually preferred to address problems as they arose, not in the abstract, but she decided to play along. "OK, since you'll have to tell them tomorrow at your conference anyway, why don't you practice on me. I'm the CEO. In your opinion, Robert, what is the mission of Chip Tronix?"

Bob smiled at her challenge, but didn't answer. Instead, he began to sketch on his note pad.

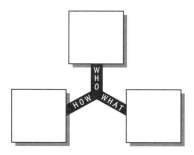

He stared at the boxes. How could he fill them in? What were the answers? He knew the answers for his team's project, or at least some of them. But with all of the changes lately at the corporate level, Bob was stymied as to the direction of Chip Tronix. "This might take some time," he concluded.

Jessica stopped role playing and said, "Bob, I'm concerned about where your company is heading. I'm not saying this because you can't fill out that chart. I know your group will do fine. You always have a way of getting the best out of people and helping them perform when the chips are down. But I'm not convinced the company has the same level of commitment for you and your group, as you have for it."

"Yeah, I know what you mean," Bob squirmed in his seat. "But this company has been around for twenty years. Our chip-building foundry is leading edge. Even without inventing our own chips to sell, we certainly could make it by just being a custom chip production company." He stayed on the defensive. He had faith in Chip Tronix, unlike many ill-chosen start-ups where he had worked earlier in his career.

"So in six months to a year, let's say, there are unforeseen circumstances and you become just a custom chip production company — which you say is the worst case. How many custom chip production companies need an R & D department?" Jessica asked.

Bob could see the vultures circling overhead. She had him dead-to-rights. Jessica must have been doing some serious thinking during her run. Yet he had faith in his company. Why couldn't she?

"Well, you're right, I suppose. But what can I do about it?" he defended himself. "This job supports us financially, with good hours, no long trips, dependable days off, telecommuting if the kids are sick. They treat me pretty well."

"I know they do. And I know you enjoy working with your team, and that guy in Des Moines…at corporate…your friend…you know, the guy from Carnegie-Melon." She had cast the line in the water, but he held off on biting to let her suffer awhile.

"Lloyd," he mercifully gave her the name.

"Yea right, Lloyd. Thank you," Jessica said. "But if those guys at corporate scrub this last-ditch effort to make this one remaining R & D project work, you're out of a job, and we're looking — again. Your whole team is looking again. We both know how much fun that is." She wasn't pleading. She wanted him to have an opportunity to reap the financial rewards he had never attained but certainly had worked for. He always got the critical elements together for a job to work, yet was rarely recognized or rewarded for those efforts. The venture capitalists and founders always came first, not the ones who made it happen.

Jessica thought now was the right time to discuss what had been bothering her for quite awhile. "Hey, we've got some good things going for us right now. The kids are both in school. I just landed that new account with the University Medical Center. Maybe we've got some flexibility here for you to do what you really want to do," she suggested.

"I am doing what I really want to do," he retorted, anxious

that she didn't share his optimism.

"I know you are," she calmly invoked confidence. "But if you have to change jobs again in six months, then we're not providing for your long-term happiness and stability — are we?"

Her logic was indisputable. But he had to believe his project would pull the company from some rough times and lead to long-term stability. After all, the neural net chip they were creating would give computers the processing ability to allow sight, hearing, touch, and smell. The neural nets could process information through multiple processors as entire sets of data, rather than the single bits flying through a single processor one at a time. This was Star Trek territory! Once the chip was made, its applications would only be limited by the creativity of the human imagination.

Jessica interrupted his daydream defense. "You know, you're always crusading about the company and, now, the company's mission. What is *Bob's* mission?" She reached over and poked his side.

"My mission," Bob leaned back, surprised by the question.

"Well yes. It seems to me if you can figure out the mission for *your* company, then you can figure out your own. So what is *your* mission? What is it that you absolutely *must* do, or what is it that you *could* do? It's that vision thing again."

"Well that's easy enough." Bob began to see the answer unfold in front of him as he wrote in his organizer. "One mission for the company; one mission for me." He bounced the tip of his pen to emphasize his completion.

COMPANY   ME

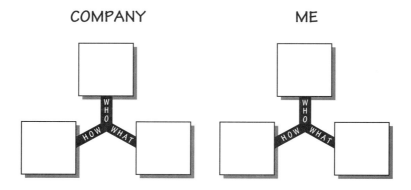

Jessica turned her focus to the traffic as they approached the exit ramp to the airport. The civilized traffic flows ended and total chaos began. Cars everywhere jockeyed for position in the four hundred feet before the roadway split into separate tracks around the airport – arrivals, departures, and parking.

A Camry cut in front of their mini-van. Jessica quickly and smoothly applied the brakes, suppressing her desire to swerve right where a bus had gradually moved along side them. Jessica breathed relief and refocused on her objective of getting two lanes over to the right — "Departures." A taxi quickly closed in from the rear. She slowed to get behind the bus. A blaring horn greeted them — the same impatient taxi.

"Hey, I'm doing the best I can!" she shouted, then smiled as she waved at him through her mirror.

"Use your signal," Bob offered, then retracted. "Sorry. I'll clear for you on your right." He looked over his shoulder for oncoming traffic, hoping to be forgiven for his unwelcome intrusion.

Jessica ignored his comment, obviously more concerned with the task at hand. "What is the deal with these people? We all have to change lanes," Jessica sounded exasperated. "We're all trying to get to the same place. We sure don't have any shared vision here. Like this guy in the silver Camaro — hey, buddy, how about letting me in?" Her best smile pointed his way. "Driving here is like your conference call yesterday. I guess the idea of shared vision may have made it into some business circles, but not at Chip Tronix and certainly not with this Camaro."

"You're right. Traffic can be like work. We're all trying to get somewhere and we need others to help us. Yet, it's kill or be killed. He's going to let you over." The Camaro had eased back.

Finally, they were in the right lane. Bob reflected on the Camaro driver's actions. The driver had let *his* vision accommodate *their* vision. This allowed all of them to get where they wanted to go. The Camaro driver had permitted shared vision to occur.

"I think shared vision is so illusive because it takes courage and patience to produce," Bob suggested. "A person has to take responsibility for enforcing the group's values so that the group can succeed. While the group may value money, information, or saving time as a final result, it takes a combination of values to get to that end. The group as a whole must value things like honesty, punctuality, respect, the customer, good service, product quality, or whatever allows it to be uniquely successful. Just like the Camaro driver. He recognized that getting everyone to the proper lane required the diligence of every driver, including himself. He applied group values to himself, and when the group succeeded, he succeeded. Indeed, when the group succeeds, every individual succeeds. But if the group fails, such as in a 20-car pile up, then everyone fails. It seems to me that once the group determines its values, everyone should want to enforce them."

Bob glanced at his note pad. If the company allowed the individual to perform his or her personal mission, and the individual contributed to the company by performing its mission and values...

"That's it! Shared vision." Bob bounced his pen repeatedly on his note pad. "That's why people don't get along at work. We say it's poor communication skills, or it's poor tracking software, or it's lack of leadership. Those might be true. But at the core of it all, we don't have shared vision!"

Now parked at the curb, Jessica could relax enough to look at Bob's note pad.

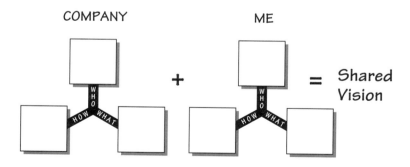

She nodded her approval at the diagram. "When you find the answers and fill in those six boxes, you'll have *your* shared vision," she said.

"You know," she continued, "if you could get people to answer their own three boxes, as well as their perspective on the group's three boxes, you could clearly see the details required to achieve shared vision."

Jessica was on a roll and Bob wanted to take full advantage. "So how do you get the answers to these six boxes?" he asked.

Jessica scanned the parking zone to ensure it was safe to ignore their allotted three minutes. It looked clear, so she decided to finish the conversation.

"Well, maybe I've gotten ahead of myself," Jessica confessed. "I want you to be happy in the long run. To do that, I think you should consider a few things. First, what do you want to do or accomplish over, say, the next five years? Second, what do you want from this company over the same five years? And finally, what do you think the company needs to do to survive, even prosper, over those five years?"

She was tired of Bob putting in terrific efforts for companies, only to see them fail because of poor decision-making at higher levels. She wanted him to include the values of those at higher levels when considering which company to work for.

Bob recorded the questions as she said them.

1. **What do you want to accomplish in the next five years?**
2. **What do you want from your company over the next five years?**
3. **What will your company need to do to survive and prosper over the next five years?**

"OK. I'll consider it. Do you want answers now?" he asked, knowing she did.

"Well, I do, but it may take awhile. Take some time on this trip to find *your* answers. When you get back, we can discuss your thoughts and find a company that's appropriate for you."

He reviewed the three questions on the note pad, written directly below his shared vision diagram. He began reading them aloud. "What do I want to accomplish over the next five years?" His eyes shifted off the sketch and back to the question. He smirked and turned toward Jessica. "You know of course what you've just asked me?"

"Yeah, I've asked you to get your act together," she said, smiling.

"No, really, you've asked me for two of the six boxes. Question number one is really — *what* should I do over the next five years? And question number three is really — *what* should the company do over the next five years? Look." Bob wrote questions one and three next to their appropriate boxes in the diagram, then pointed at the two questions with the tip of his pen while explaining the correlation.

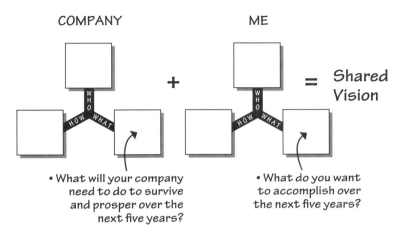

COMPANY   ME

+   = Shared Vision

• What will your company   • What do you want
need to do to survive   to accomplish over
and prosper over the   the next five years?
next five years?

"Yes, come to think of it, you're right," Jessica smiled again.

Bob felt happy this was all coming together, but it still left one question. He now returned the tip of his pen to question number two. Perhaps Jessica could explain its importance. "I don't know the significance of the second question."

She asked him to reread the question. "What do I want from the company over those five years?"

Jessica thought quietly, then had the answer. "Well, if the company is successful at its mission, which you contributed to, then you should expect the company to reasonably provide you with what you wanted in your answers to question two. That way, you can continue to stay and contribute, and the company can continue to perform its mission. Likewise, if you don't contribute to the direction of the company, the company shouldn't be expected to provide you with what you want. They should be expected to fire you."

"So you're saying it's a two-way street. If I help the company provide for its mission, the company should help me with mine, and vice-versa. Moreover, the company should consider me part of its mission, and I should consider it part of mine. Is there anything really new there?"

"There is. You wondered why everyone was always building their résumés or empires in the vicious cycle. The reason is because no one is formally defining responsibility and linking it to both parties. For instance, if an individual can't meet her mission because the company doesn't support it, she's gone — jumps ship. The company loses intellectual capital and the employee loses a secure job. Similarly, if the company can't succeed at its mission, then it can't provide for the individual. Once again, the employee must look for other means to accomplish her mission." Jessica took Bob's pen and drew arrows on his chart. "With shared vision, the individual is responsible for the group's success, and the group is responsible for the individual's success."

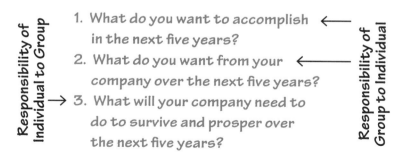

"OK, so back to the mission boxes." Bob wanted to see how this responsibility issue played on his boxes. "Is it, therefore, the responsibility of both parties to seek completion of each of the six boxes?"

"Sure, since both parties need to accomplish their missions on a continual basis, shared vision requires each to contribute to the other," Jessica replied.

"So I need to find the questions that allow me to fill in the boxes. Then both parties can help each other arrive at shared vision," Bob responded.

"That's it. Not only for the company, but for you." She was pleased to see him considering his future so intently. Finally, he was placing equal value on what *he* needed to do in his life, not just what the *company* needed him to do.

Bob added the "responsibility arrows" to his shared vision diagram.

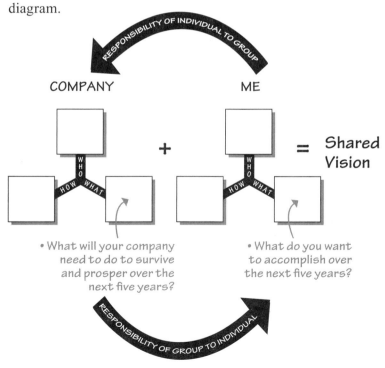

"Wow! This is great stuff." Jessica's ideas sincerely energized Bob . . . so much so that he had lost track of time. They'd been talking quite a while, and he now felt that unsettling feeling of "being late." He forced himself not to panic. Jessica immediately saw his uneasiness with being late and had to swallow a laugh.

"Thanks for the ride. Date night when I get back?" he asked, then leaned and kissed her before hopping out of the van and grabbing his luggage.

"You bet. Good luck on your quest for shared vision. I can't wait to see what you find out. Call me tonight."

Jessica pulled away from the curb. Bob began his search for shared vision.

CHAPTER **4**

Illusive
Corporate Targets

THE LINE AT THE TICKET COUNTER WAS A FOOTBALL FIELD long. International Airways had three huge counters at San Francisco, each with more than 25 agents. Signs above the agents indicated the function of each of the counters. Bob walked past the first counter and stretched to see the signs over the crowd. The agents' signs read: 'First Class/Business Class.' "Great," he thought, wondering where the 'Coach' people went. He saw another lobby area about two hundred feet away and walked toward it. This lobby was filled with another long line and a second army of agents with signs that said: 'Purchase Tickets.' It would have been nice if the signs out on the curb reflected the type of service inside, rather than just the airline's name. After a second hike, he found himself in the third lobby reading a sign that said: 'Passengers with Tickets, Baggage

Check-In.' The line here was just as overwhelming. Why every flight heading east had to leave at 9:00 a.m. was beyond him. This was simply another case of how the system was bigger than any individual airline or customer.

An attendant greeted Bob as he entered the line, "Do you have your ticket, sir?" Bob answered yes and moved into the cordoned amusement-park-like maze.

A young woman, dwarfed by two very heavy and unruly pieces of luggage, entered the line behind him. Momentum looked to be in her favor to this point, so stopping to answer the customer service agent's questions meant losing some serious kinetic energy. But the agent dutifully stopped the woman to ensure she was entering the correct line.

Bob couldn't hear the conversation but clearly saw the disappointment on the young woman's face when she learned she had to go to the 'Purchase Tickets' counter several hundred feet away.

The young woman came out of her bag-lugging crouch. She allowed her sizable purse and computer case to drop sharply off their balanced positions on her shoulders, free falling until their straps jarred her wrists. "Ouch," Bob cringed, "that had to hurt." The young woman attempted to talk the agent into letting her be the exception to the rule and enter the line for the sake of heavy bag management. Not possible. Disgust registered all over her face as the agent's arm stretched toward the proper line a terminal length away.

Bob knew the power of rules and the structure of processes well. No matter what supervisory positions he held, he always had a love/hate relationship with organizational structure. So many times, he relied on the company's structure to provide his team the support they needed with equipment maintenance, legal issues, pay and benefits, and strategic direction. The things he valued frequently aligned with what the organization seemed to value as well. The company's structure provided such a security blanket when compared with the rigors of entrepreneurship. Yet, whenever he had difficulty motivating, retaining, or promoting employees, the structure wouldn't budge to allow for the needs of the individual to be met. Likewise, removing deadbeat employees required superhuman efforts and a complete understanding of organizational procedure. In either case, organizational values proved inflexible when the needs of the individual called for flexibility.

This situation at International's ticket counter was yet another example of structured efficiency not meeting the needs of individuals. Sure, the airline provided better service for its customers departing San Francisco by setting up different locations for specific services. Obviously, this three-lobby process of checking in passengers didn't happen by chance. It was the result of considerable experience and process improvement. Most likely, it came directly from people who worked with the process everyday: the customer service agents. The experts, right?

Yet, Bob saw that about every tenth customer showed up in the wrong line. Were the customers wrong to be upset to learn of their new decathlon challenge? And being the customer service agent at the end of the line had to be a challenge as well. How would you like to tell overburdened customers they chose incorrectly? How often do you get a happy response in that situation? Bob thought they must have to rotate that job, or give it to the "new guy" every month. Did the customer service experts take note of International's rise in unhappy customers and employees? Certainly International's values weren't being met here either.

This check-in line was just another example of people waking up happy in the morning and disliking each other by the end of the day. It was not through any defiant action of their own, but by having to enter relationships governed by an organizational structure that prohibited the satisfaction of their personal values. The young woman who hadn't seen this check-in process unhappily learned she had selected the wrong terminal door. The customer service agent was unhappy to be delivering bad news for the hundredth time that morning. Each person became unhappy with the other because of a situation forcibly repeated dozens of times a day. The culprit: design of a process that didn't consider organizational values.

Bob watched another customer receive the finger of destiny now. Once again, the long look of despair crossed this man's face. Bob had a simple solution. Because the lines are so long, and the number of people overwhelming, it's nearly impossible to clearly see the agents' counter signs. Make these signs bigger and higher. In addition, the lack of signs the airport authority provided on the drop-off curb set everyone up for failure. Add more signs. He decided he might as well inform the ticket agent of his insight.

"Next in line, please."

"Next in line, sir!!" the agent repeated herself.

Bob had become the next in line. He apologized to no one in particular for day dreaming, then dragged his bag to the counter. The ticket agent greeted Bob cordially and was pleased to see he already had his identification and e-ticket itinerary out. Her goldplated nametag read Kathleen. "Just one bag today to Des Moines, Mr. Sippel?"

"Yes, thank you. Can you confirm I'm in an aisle seat, and my frequent flyer number is logged for this flight?"

"It is," she strained, looking at the screen for a hidden number. "You're all set, Flight 200 to Chicago, then on to Des Moines. Seat 19G, an aisle seat, and you're at Gate 84."

"Thank you, Kathleen." Bob always made it a point to try and use people's names. In an impersonal world, it made life a bit more personal. "I couldn't help but notice the number of people who try to enter the wrong line." Bob pointed to the end of the line. "Your agents then have to pass along the bad news and direct them to another line. It seems to me, you just need to install more informative signs in your lobbies and some signs out front to better direct people. It might ease some tensions."

Kathleen was wearing a pleasant customer service smile. Bob couldn't tell if she was hiding an "I've heard this all before look," or if she was really interested in his comment.

"I know. We've tried signs before but had problems. The airport authority has rules about posting signs both inside and out. I'll certainly mention this to our customer service experts. Thank you, Mr. Sippel. Next in line, please!"

Bob resented the "next in line, please" brush-off. He

wasn't going to push the issue, though. He had a plane to catch and not much time to do it. He somehow had become uncharacteristically late.

Bob started the Olympic speed walk to Gate 84. He couldn't stand poor customer service, and often challenged himself to find a solution as if he were the manager in such a situation. Who does the airline serve? he thought. Well, obviously the customer, of which he's one. So why couldn't they change something so simple, yet so important? He surely wasn't the first to recommend such a change. Why wasn't it fixed?

Both the passengers and International Airways needed a solution. The customers had identified the problem, so who was responsible for fixing it? Bob began to consider the other players who had a stake in the problem. It could be a *supplier* issue. The airport authority — the supplier in this case — holds a significant stake in the solution. Not only did they control signage for International, but for all of the other airlines. Speaking of other airlines, they must have these problems as well. So *competitors* also had an interest in the solution. Perhaps all the airlines collectively could approach the airport and demand change. Bob was surprised at the number of players who potentially had a stake in this.

He wondered who else could help. Bob had just finished a book called *Co-opetition* that suggested businesses not in the same field could actually improve sales and service by working together. So who complements baggage check-in? he pondered. Maybe, the sky caps and traffic cops. Perhaps if International Airways helped them by paying for general customer service training, they could help International by getting people through the choke points to the correct places. Happier customers for International, better trained sky caps and traffic cops, improved customer service. Certainly this noncompetitive relationship wouldn't threaten either of them and could benefit both.

I guess there's a lot that could be done, Bob concluded. A company needs to look at more than just the customer to determine who they serve. They need to consider everyone they work with — in each of the tasks they conduct. In the case of checking in passengers, International could improve customer service by working with the supplier (airport authority), the competitors (other airlines), and the complementary relationships (sky caps, traffic cops, etc.).

"Now boarding all rows for Flight 200 to Chicago," the announcement rose above the din of the terminal.

Even in the hurried bustle of dodging the beeping carts and other frantic travelers, the parallel hit him. The problem facing International while checking in passengers was no different than the problem Chip Tronix had defining its mission. When considering *who* we serve, we must consider everyone we work with.

There were many open seats in the boarding area at Gate 84. Bob grabbed one. He wanted to add another question to the boxes.

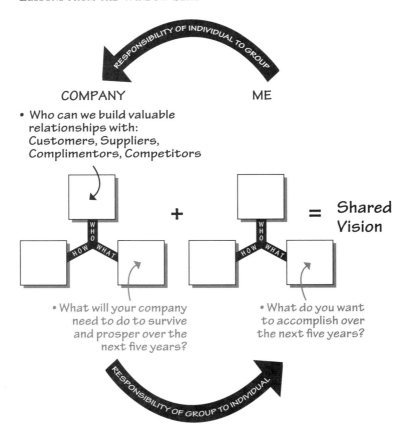

COMPANY

ME

- Who can we build valuable relationships with: Customers, Suppliers, Complimentors, Competitors

+

=

Shared Vision

• What will your company need to do to survive and prosper over the next five years?

• What do you want to accomplish over the next five years?

Bob sat reflecting on his work when he heard, "Final call for Flight 200." He slapped his personal organizer shut and hurriedly headed for the gate. He scolded himself for not paying more attention to the flight announcements; even the flight attendants seemed to be waiting for him.

Finding the other three questions for the other three boxes dominated his thoughts.

PART **II**

WHEN
VALUES
ALIGN

CHAPTER **5**

Retaining Valued Employees

T HE FUSELAGE DOOR SHUT BEHIND HIM. AS HE WALKED DOWN the aisle, Bob felt all eyes on him. He had never before been the last one on board, and he didn't like it. It was easy to find his seat. It was the only empty one. He shoved his briefcase in an overhead bin and quickly sat down while giving an apologetic smile to the woman in the window seat next to him. He needed to remember to adjust his schedule next time to accommodate the crush of travelers for 9:00 a.m. flights. This was a little too close.

Bob's head sunk into the headrest. Ahhhhh, a 777. Even a coach seat was like business class on any other airplane. Boeing did it right when they made this plane. Any other plane in the fleet and his knees would be sharply pressing into the kidneys of the person in front of him. And forget arm room. Even simple tasks like turning the pages of the newspaper required the assistance of the person in the middle seat. But the 777 was different. Lots of room. Plenty of televisions to watch and a personal audio system with real headphones, not the air tube version.

Bob smiled at the woman next to him and cordially asked, "Hello. Where are you headed?"

She responded, "Chicago," but didn't elaborate. It became apparent to Bob she was more interested in reading her magazine than talking. Bob obliged.

He looked for a distraction to whittle away the time. The *Great Circle* in-flight magazine with a beautiful fishing stream on the cover caught his eye. Bob liked to peruse the in-flight magazines for vacation ideas. Pictures of far away beaches and golf resorts stimulated carefree daydreaming.

Bob flipped the pages effortlessly. *Why Employees Leave Their Employers* — a title that sparked his interest. "Wonder if this is similar to what Jess was talking about this morning?" This boxed area caught his eye:

> **Employees are most likely to leave a new company within 21 weeks of being hired.**

"I've been reading the same article," the woman next to him suddenly said. "I normally don't read these in-flight magazines, but this article is quite interesting, don't you think?"

Bob turned to face her. "I haven't started the article. What's it about?" he asked.

"Well, it explains exactly why people leave work. First, it lists the top ten reasons employees move on to a new job. The top three reasons all have to do with values."

"Values and not money?" Bob questioned.

"No, money comes fifth on the list. The article claims that satisfying our core values is what does the trick. Things like open and honest communication, control over work, and the nature of work itself — whatever is most important to you. If your values mesh with those of both your job and your group, then you're an unusually lucky and probably very happy employee. Let me show you." She pointed to the next page where there were four names listed, with a paragraph next to each name.

"The author has the readers do this exercise where you become the Human Resources Director. The 'boss' is concerned about four people in your organization and wants you to predict if they'll stay or leave the firm. You determine if you'll have to replace these folks over the coming months. The goal is to figure out who will stay and who will go relative to values achievement." She pointed to a graph that showed whether or not both the company and employee were achieving their respective values . . . if they were "winning."

Company's Values

	Lose	Win
Worker's Values — Lose	Lose	Win
Worker's Values — Win	Lose	Win

"Got it?" the woman asked.

"OK, let's try it," Bob responded.

"**Bill** is our first subject. Bill is a great guy to have lunch with. He's energetic and always has a joke — once you're away from the office. However, he doesn't do a lot of work in or out of the office. You can always count on his availability for lunch! Lately, Bill expressed to you that, while the pay is good, he doesn't feel the organization knows what his skills are. The company doesn't allow him to perform to his maximum level. Since his talents are underused, Bill thinks the boss doesn't like him.

"The second guy is **Ralph**. Ralph is a hard charger. Lists of accomplishments line his performance reports. A year ago, Ralph was promoted to head the 15-person sales department. Shortly after the promotion, though, Ralph's department wasn't making its projected goals. Recently, several sales people confessed to you that Ralph wants them to lie on their end-of-month reports. Ralph rationalized that the ill-reported excesses will be more than compensated for when they 'sign the big account.' You've also noticed that, since taking over the department, Ralph is sometimes 'rough around the edges' in dealing with subordinates. Though you hear occasional rumblings of salespersons threatening to quit, the boss doesn't seem to want to help Ralph with interpersonal skills development. Ralph continues to ride roughshod over his troops so he can make sales quotas and achieve his bonus.

"Next is **Donna**. You recruited Donna to the company six months ago. Her expertise in production design is well known among the competitors in the industry. Fortunately, she and her husband wanted to move to your area this past year, and you made her an offer she couldn't refuse. Product quality and production rates have improved steadily since Donna joined the production staff. She advised her team that she must leave everyday at 5 P.M. to pick up her children, but she has a mobile phone if any 'after hours' questions arise. Recently, the boss told Donna that, when the company signs the 'big account,' she'll need to stay at the office later to make ends meet without an increase in staff. Otherwise, he'll be forced to replace her. Donna already created the designs necessary to satisfy the new workload should the 'big account' be signed, but she'll need to hire three more people, which the boss said she couldn't do. Donna approached you as a friend, and told you she is torn between her family and work.

"Finally, there's **Francisco**. Francisco has been with the company since its inception. In fact, when the boss started his product line, Francisco's R & D group created three straight winners. Francisco has read extensively about customer service over the years. He regularly meets with department heads, salespeople, marketing reps, customers, and suppliers to determine their unfulfilled needs. He shares his findings with his group and uses its ingenuity to develop products that help the company prosper. Francisco also regularly plays racquetball with the boss. During that forum, he discusses the needs R & D will have in creating new products. Amazingly, those needs always make it into the budget."

The woman looked up at Bob and asked, "What do you think?"

After several seconds, Bob answered. "I think Donna will

leave, Ralph will get fired, Francisco will definitely stay, and Bill will probably just leach off of the company for years to come."

"Well, you're pretty close." She gave him a surprised grin. "Remember how I said everything went back to values? Now try to place each person in the diagram." She turned the page and pointed.

Bob pulled out a pen and filled in the chart.

Company's Values

	Lose	Win
Lose (Worker's Values)	Lose Bill	Win Donna
Win (Worker's Values)	Lose Ralph	Win Francisco

"That's right. When we place each of the four examples in a box, we can see whether their values and the company's values are being satisfied at work.

"So Bill, though always available for lunch, isn't satisfied personally nor is the company benefiting to the fullest extent from his employment.

"In this 'Lose/Lose' work environment, he will most likely leave when he recognizes how stagnant he is. Donna loses if she stays because her family life would suffer, but the company would win. Ralph is happy with his situation, but the company is losing with ill-reported sales and unhappy subordinates. Ralph will most likely be forced out as he doesn't share the company's values. Francisco and the company are obviously both winning. Francisco will be with the company a long time."

Bob's seatmate really enjoyed both the article and telling him about it. He had learned early on from Jessica not to stop someone who is on a roll. The woman continued, "Whenever a worker's values aren't satisfied, that person *will* leave the company. Ultimately, we will all leave if we can't be fulfilled. Likewise, when the company's values aren't upheld like in Ralph's situation, he'll be fired or asked to leave.

"The article goes on to say that as soon as you know your values differ from the company's, you immediately look to change jobs — regardless of how long it takes you to actually leave. So companies having difficulty retaining valued employees — their so-called 'intellectual capital'— need to ensure that company and personal values are aligned."

She pointed to the bottom right square on the last graph. "Only groups that have the group's values aligned with each employee's values have true teamwork. Teamwork simply isn't possible for the misaligned pairings. In these three situations, workers may come to work and form a work group, but their preoccupation with achieving personal goals will ultimately prohibit the group's total success. Only when a worker's values tie into the direction of the group can he or she care about the

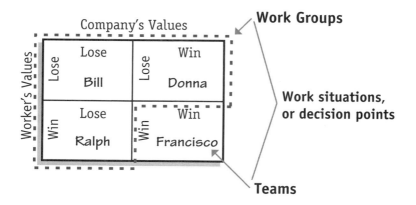

group as much as about self." She laid her hand palm down on the magazine as if to signal the close of the article.

"So if I recognize that my core needs and values, 'who I am' so to speak, are in conflict with or not supported by the company, I might as well resign right then?" Bob asked as if unsure of himself.

"Well, it doesn't say to quit right away, but it does say you'll eventually leave unless values are brought into alignment." She confirmed the answer to his question.

"So if companies need to ensure employee values are upheld in the workplace...if they plan to retain employees and not fire them...then they better talk to the employees to find out what gives," Bob conjectured. "It's as if the employees are customers and suppliers at the same time. Align values or lose the account."

"You've got it," she confirmed.

Bob reflected on the revelation they had just made. The company or group needed to consider the employee just as much as any customer or supplier. Was it possible? Did companies serve their employees as well as their customers? Bob knew how hard it was to find engineers who did neural net construction. Retaining them was a problem. Should he formally consider the values of the employees? So many had left to start their own companies or contribute to the efforts of other start-ups. Maybe it took more than simply offering a competitive salary and benefits. Maybe it was about respect for ideas and values.

Bob pulled out his note pad and quickly added to it.

COMPANY   ME

- Who can we build valuable
  relationships with:
  Customers, Suppliers,
  Complimentors, Competitors
- Who are our team
  members? Are we
  considering their values?

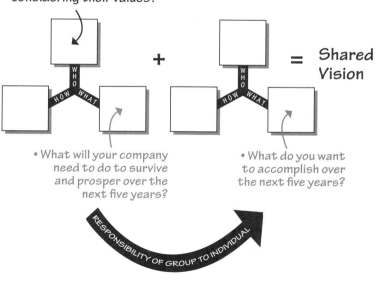

+   = Shared
                                             Vision

• What will your company
  need to do to survive
  and prosper over the
  next five years?

• What do you want
  to accomplish over
  the next five years?

CHAPTER **6**

The Glue
in Collaboration

B OB BID A CORDIAL "SEE YOU LATER" TO HIS SEATMATE AS
she left the plane in Chicago. He wished he could have
such an interesting travel companion on every trip. Bob
didn't have to change planes, so he decided to take a quick nap
during the loading and unloading phases.

Some thirty minutes passed before Bob awoke to a
disturbance in the row in front of him. A young man had
approached a gentleman in the aisle seat and said, "Excuse
me, I think you're in my seat." The two compared boarding
passes and both had rights to seat 18H. They summoned a flight
attendant. She explained that, on such a full flight, she couldn't
reseat the young man until the door was closed. "Could you
please return to the gate agent for a new seat assignment?" she

asked. The young man dejectedly headed back toward the front of the plane and the flight attendant walked away.

Another flight attendant, whose nametag read Janet, was packing overhead compartments and briefly stopped what she was doing. She calmly whispered "Rebecca" while subtly tilting her head toward the jetway door. Janet's raised eyebrows clearly said, "Don't just stand there, go with him." Rebecca received the message loud and clear. She hurried up the jetway to catch the young man and take care of the problem for him.

The situation didn't seem like much, Bob thought, but he had witnessed a marvelous display of teamwork. Janet kept at her task of securing the cabin, while aiding Rebecca with her customer service skills.

What if the customer service agents at the 'Passengers with Tickets' counter had displayed the same level of customer service? Bob suspected that if this problem happened at the ticket counter, it would have gone unnoticed. Even if a ticketing supervisor had noticed, she probably would have just stepped in, taken control, and solved the problem. But here a coworker made an impact on Rebecca's behavior without taking control of the situation. Why was it then that coworkers had more impact on team member performance than bosses did? Bob wondered. Maybe because employees really do the work and don't want to clean up other people's messes, especially customer service messes, he surmised.

Just yesterday, his friend Lloyd brought up the topic of team member communication while talking on the phone. Lloyd was reflecting on a team-building course he had participated in.

He, and each of the other participants, had to fall backwards into a semicircle of participants who then caught them with their outstretched arms. The point was, of course, that you can only take risks with the backing of your team. You have to trust them to catch you when you fall. Yet, in his marketing department, Lloyd pointed out an employee worked alone ninety percent of the time. The other ten percent seemed to be simply wasted in team meetings. There were no outstretched arms between the office partitions. There were goals and quotas, and individuals responsible for meeting them, but no cushioned recovery when someone fell short. "How do you make the jump from individuals with goals, quotas, and responsibilities, to teams that perform leaps of faith?" Lloyd posed.

The flight attendant Janet had just answered Lloyd's question. Individuals can perform leaps of faith when they know the organization's values will support them. Rather than reflect on what they individually wanted to do, Janet and Rebecca together did what would be best for the airline and its customers. They used the airline's values to provide priority and direction. The flight attendants didn't do each other's work. They helped each other by giving nonbinding suggestions, just like astronauts doing a space walk or basketball players during a time out.

In this example, the leap of faith did not mean taking unfounded risk into the unknown. The leap of faith was trusting a coworker to steer another down the right path. If each team member, bringing different talents and insights to the team, could believe that other team members have his or her best interest at heart, then Lloyd's question was answered.

Bob got out his organizer and made a note to tell Lloyd about this revelation.

Team values are the glue that hold teams together and guide them in the proper direction.

The flight attendants showed that:

1. Even when working alone, an individual can benefit by being on a team.

2. Likewise, both the team and the team members can improve performance when an individual elects to participate on a team.

3. Being on a team does not mean being together all of the time in order to accomplish tasks — as we've been led to believe.

The obvious question Lloyd would ask next is: "How then do we get team members, including the empire builders, to trust each other?" It was a huge question. Bob didn't have a clue how to answer it as he leaned back against the headrest.

The plane was finally loaded and everyone seated. The jetway door closed. Bob shut his eyes as the plane backed up, and sleep soon came.

After a while, Bob was jerked awake by the beverage cart grazing his shoulder. "I'm sorry, sir," Janet said with an apologetic hand on his shoulder. "Sometimes the turbulence gives these carts a mind of their own. May I get you something to drink?"

"Yes, please. Diet Coke." Bob rubbed his eyes as he rejoined the conscious world.

"And you, sir?" The question went to the gentleman now in

the window seat. "Lite beer, please." He handed her a twenty.

Janet turned to her serving partner across the well-laden drink cart and asked, "I'm out of ones. Do you have change?"

Rebecca quickly responded as if to show off her preparedness. "Oh sure, I always stock up on small bills before a flight."

"That would be a first for me." Janet smiled as if to compliment Rebecca. The two got along quite well even though this seemed to be their first flight together. Bob was even more perplexed about their friendly relationship when he considered their differing personalities and priorities.

Bob sipped his Diet Coke and pondered how two strangers could immediately fall into such a pleasant working environment. In contrast, the upper management at Chip Tronix regularly plotted against each other. Janet and Rebecca demonstrated different talents and values throughout the trip, but liked and respected each other more because of them. How could Chip Tronix do that?

Bob caught Janet's attention as the lite beer passed across him. "Do they stress some sort of customer service credo or set of values in your training? I've noticed that you two have different styles that complement each other well."

"No, sir. We spent most of our training learning the different aircraft and their safety systems. They didn't devote a lot of time to customer service, though we did get some basic training. I don't remember a credo or anything like that."

"Hmmm. That's interesting. I really thought you did a good

job handling the 'same seat' problem earlier." Bob handed out compliments quite naturally.

"Thank you," Janet said sincerely before moving on to the next row.

Apparently, International Airways had no real plan for sharing values in the workplace, yet everyone obviously benefited when shared values were in place.

Shared values would have been helpful in many of the day's situations: at the check-in line, on the airport off ramp, on the conference call, and in the vicious cycle. Yet there was no real stimulus to achieve them. He saw that only a waning sense of common decency stood in the way of complete anarchy.

When Bob took over the R & D department a year ago, he called his work group together to talk about what each expected of the group. Bob thought he'd cut through all of his people's pet peeves to avoid any childish arguments down the road. But now, after seeing the flight attendants work together, he realized the meeting had been much more meaningful. Timeliness, honesty, no pager beeps during meetings, no interrupting each other while working on the computer, no remarks of sexual nature in the workplace, no calls at home, etc. All of these were the values each expected of the others so they could work together. It was their credo. A credo they updated as team members came and left the group. It worked because it reflected the values of the current group, not those of any outsider.

Bob pulled out his organizer again. He reviewed his diagram. He began to realize the *how* box for the company had a two-part answer. Half of reaching the mission objective was in the performance of the task itself, the actual approach used in making the product or service...be it simple problem-solving or ISO 9000 process improvement. There was "a way" to do a task, and probably a company policy letter could spell out the procedure. He added this question to the Company's *how* box.

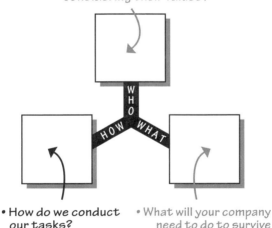

COMPANY

• Who can we build valuable relationships with: Customers, Suppliers, Complimentors, Competitors
• Who are our team members? Are we considering their values?

• How do we conduct our tasks?

• What will your company need to do to survive and prosper over the next five years?

The other half of *how* to get things done concerned the process of working together. What values encouraged performance? What values prohibited it? If a team planned on working together for any period of time, they'd have to use their group values to define acceptable individual conduct, just as the magazine article emphasized with the Sales Manager, Ralph. When Ralph didn't support or uphold the group values, he was fired.

Group values provide the lubrication for the gears to turn. The group's values — in performing the process of work — hold the team members to an agreed-upon standard of conduct, just as Bob's project team had determined. Honesty, timeliness, no interruptions while on the computer, etc. These were the laws of interpersonal conduct for Bob's team, determined and enforced only by themselves. Certainly, the team's ownership of these laws meant they would likely be used and upheld, unlike so many company policies that didn't affect anyone personally.

The importance of group values in conducting operations seemed so obvious now. "But, do companies really establish and hold themselves accountable to group values?" Bob's skepticism surfaced. "Well, if they are going to achieve shared vision, they must," he answered his own question. The answer left him uncomfortable. He was beginning to abandon the safety net of corporate structure in favor of using a system of group values.

It couldn't be. "Aren't the company's policies important things to uphold?" Then it hit him, "The company's polices should only be upheld when they don't conflict with the company's values. The International Airways' agent had chosen *policy* over *value* with the young woman in the check-in line. At the check-in counter, Kathleen had chosen policy over value."

Bob flipped back to his original diagram and added the

question of group values to the company's *how* box. If shared vision was going to occur, he'd have to uphold group values as staunchly as his own. Just as the Camaro driver had done earlier in the day.

Before today, he would never have ranked the company's values on par with his own. He had better start.

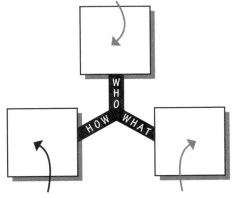

COMPANY

• Who can we build valuable relationships with: Customers, Suppliers,

• Who are our team members? Are we considering their values?

• How do we conduct our tasks?

• What values encourage or prohibit performance?

• What will your company need to do to survive and prosper over the next five years?

CHAPTER **7**

Why
I Work

THE AIRPORT ARRIVAL EXPERIENCE WAS AS PAINLESS AS possible. Bob had gone from the jetway to starting his rental car in just thirty minutes. That had to be a new Sippel record.

Before he knew it, he had entered the hotel. It had a beautiful atrium lobby. The lobby was located on the second floor and overlooked a restaurant and bar. The atrium over the bar area was encircled by glass, almost as if it were a green house that happened to be the size of a gymnasium. The bar itself was quite long and was staffed by a number of bartenders. While Bob took in the view from the registration counter, five of the bartenders jumped up on the bar, as if responding to a challenge of one of the patrons. They each grabbed an instrument from racks on the bar, which Bob thought were simply decorations, and proceeded to play dixieland jazz. What a place! If you had to have meetings, this was definitely the place.

Lloyd had suggested they meet in the bar around six. Bob's get-togethers with Lloyd always highlighted his Des Moines trips. Lloyd was great. He possessed that uncanny ability to make everyone feel valued. Every friendship, even a casual relationship, was sacred to him. From an early age, Lloyd had the vision of knowing that work and projects would always be there, but friends and acquaintances might not. Lloyd was also an expert in his life's vocation — marketing. His efforts to develop overseas markets allowed the company to become a major player in both chip design and chip set assembly. Without the international base Lloyd had developed, the investment capital simply wouldn't have been available for the company to grow as fast as it had. In work or pleasure, Lloyd uniquely lived life with a balance between *things to do* and *relationships to build.*

Bob hopped on the elevator and quickly dropped his bags in the room. It was already after 6 P.M. — time to leave a quick message for Jess, then back downstairs so he wouldn't be late for his meeting.

Bob was soon at a table with a view and ordered a draft. He wasn't surprised to see Lloyd arrive with Sharon and Terry from the office.

Sharon, a "forty-something" corporate lawyer, had put herself through law school when she was 38. She had argued in front of the state supreme court as an intern and succeeded in reversing a 100-year-old ruling! Then, in her first month as an attorney, she argued and won an intellectual property ruling at the U.S. District Court level. She had a passion for knowing her cases inside and out.

The CEO of Chip Tronix heard of Sharon's astonishing abilities and made her an offer she couldn't refuse. She later admitted the title "Director" had a nice ring to it. Though she was with the company for just over a year, Bob felt as if she had always been a friend.

Terry had been with the company since its inception twenty years ago. Her timing over the years was perfect. She performed a variety of jobs as the company grew. An accountant by profession, the company originally hired her to take care of all of the "accounting functions."

In her first month, while writing the company's checks, she quickly learned that many human resources functions were neglected. Terry felt she could make things happen for her fellow employees. She took it upon herself to research benefit packages and convinced the CEO to select one! The change made a huge difference in everyone's feelings of safety, security, and overall happiness.

The CEO recognized her passion for making things happen and put her in charge of organizing the human resources, accounting, and training departments. He even trusted her to hire the current directors of each.

She completed her MBA at night, so she could make an even bigger impact at work. Everyone respected her uniqueness as the "non-engineer" and her ability to handle issues on the spot. Respect for Terry seemed to grow and grow. In fact, when the company went public, there was no decision to make —

Terry became the CFO.

Bob stood to greet them all, immediately feeling this trip was worthwhile. Smiles were abundant. This group of four had known each other for some time and shared a friendship that had grown from mutual respect. This encounter would undoubtedly turn into "the meeting before the meeting."

"What? You didn't bring Ramin!" Bob said sarcastically. Bob knew full well that a discussion with his boss Ramin would never get past the subjects of upcoming reports and deadlines.

"No, we figured we could conduct your inquisition just fine without him," Terry replied with a warm smile. "Now," she mocked Ramin's voice, "why don't you explain last month's 1.3 percent contractor cost overrun." The group laughed.

Ramin had become more and more careless in recent months when it came to micromanagement. As VP for Operations and Research, he felt the strain of losing most of his R & D department. As the budget and his department shrank, he tightened his grip on who and what remained.

Everyone knew the budget would rebound. In fact, the marketing decision-makers had already determined that Bob's team would have the first and only neural net chip on the market. It would create a new market niche and bring in solid profits. Production of the new chip would complete one vicious cycle and start another, regardless of Ramin.

No one in this cocktail group would defend Ramin's recent micromanagement. After all, he was a big boy and should know better. He had exquisite credentials as a Ph.D. in electrical engineering and an MBA to round out his business skills. He started as a pioneer in neural net design. He had invented the theory of probabilistic neural net technology in his doctoral thesis in 1963. Only today did the hardware exist that allowed Bob's team to bring Ramin's idea to life.

No doubt about it, Ramin was the expert. His expertise had grown to, or perhaps had always been, *who he truly was.* Unfortunately, his leadership skills had regressed in recent months to a simple level of management. Management of Bob's team, for instance, had become a set of rules and demands. He ordered team members around as if they were a resource to be used, not a group of people to be emotionally replenished, fortified, and challenged. Bob had felt the pointed end of many spears from Ramin lately and everyone at the table knew it.

"Well, Bob, if it makes you feel better, even Ramin has been running some blocking for you," Sharon piped up. "Last week, Todd (the CEO) jumped around complaining to Ramin that 'the shareholders need results they can see, hear, touch and smell! If you can't make an impact on them with increased earnings this quarter, then at least give me a product to introduce at the annual meeting.' Ramin couldn't guarantee a product that soon, but he defended your team by assuring that no other chip design firm could top your team's expertise. In fact, he even said that no other company could capably venture to this product line. As inventor of the technology, he didn't see anyone more qualified to make this happen than you, Bob. He told Todd if he wanted results, he might pay your team more so they wouldn't leave the project in midstream."

"Wow, Ramin said that?" Bob was surprised and flattered.

"Yup. Sometimes Todd forgets about his open-door policy.

His assistant, Cheryl, and I got an earful while I was scheduling some meetings. By the way, none of you heard this from me or Cheryl." Sharon lifted an eyebrow and leaned toward Bob to non-verbally confirm his sworn secrecy.

Bob's smile put her at ease. "Just this morning, my wife asked me questions about what makes me tick, 'Why I Work' so to speak. Compliments like that would have to be part of the answer."

"I don't know if compliments are part of the answer for me," Sharon confessed. "Oh, sure, they're nice," she backpedaled a bit. "But I need to have control over my work. I have to be the complete master. Not allowing me the freedom to become the subject matter expert on whatever tasks I am assigned would be like a downhill racer being locked in a ski lodge with large windows. I'd be able to look at what I could do but unable to do it. For me, the project is what's most important. Yes, the people I work with are important. But it's what we come together to accomplish that's of most importance, isn't it? That's why we work, isn't it?"

Sharon knew she had asked a controversial question when it was met with silence.

Lloyd was the bravest and confessed, "Well, that's not why I work. I need this," he opened the palms of his hands to include the whole group. "It's times like these that are most important. I need to get to know the people I'm with and what they're all about. I like to act as a catalyst for personal growth so we can enjoy a better workplace, community, and, hopefully, a better world. If I had to make sales calls only from the phone in my cubicle or couldn't attend meetings and trade shows, you can forget it. I'd be out looking for a new job. I need to develop human potential. Of course, I'd like to do that and be well paid," Lloyd smiled half jokingly. "But put me in front of a computer all day and forget it — I'm gone. Sure, my family and I need the pay and benefits the company provides, but I have no reason to believe I couldn't earn similar pay and benefits elsewhere. The relationships I've built here would be the hardest part of the job to replace. If I had to leave, one of the first values I'd look to fulfill in a new company would be the potential for new relationships. Terry, how about you?"

Terry paused. "I don't know exactly. There are a lot of reasons why I work. Mostly, I need to know that I'm making a difference. The group certainly needs me, and I need the group. But, really, they need me more. If they didn't, I'd find a group that did. I also can't be tied down by rules and regulations. I've got to take a problem, solve it, and move on to the next problem, regardless of how we've done it before or what some policy letter says. If I fail, I learn from it and move on. Most of the time I don't fail. I improve the situation."

Bob interjected, "If my team fails, then I have failed. Not just as a leader either, for I had that same feeling before becoming a leader. I need to get each person involved with the group. In fact, I get uncomfortable when group members don't get along. I'm always the peacemaker. Over time, if I can't see how my contribution allows the group to succeed at its assignments, I feel ineffective and dissatisfied. When I feel the group sinking and I'm unable to help right the ship, then it's time to move on. That's it, I guess. I have to know that others need me so they can do their jobs. I need to feel valued for being part of the group, a stabilizing and contributing part."

Bob was unsettled. His answer came too easily. He didn't know if, by expressing his feelings, he was anguishing over recent short-term problems or expressing real long-term core issues. Just this morning he was unable to fill in his "mission boxes." What was so different now?

He wanted the group to help him in his quest. "You know, I think by answering this question off the cuff, I may not be giving you an accurate answer. I may just be thinking out loud. When Jessica asked me similar questions this morning, I couldn't answer them. So let me pose a few questions to the group. Why have you left jobs? We can all come up with a list of things we'd like to have in our work, but where's the line? What *must* you have at work?" Bob repeated his question. "Why have you left good or even not-so-good jobs?"

Bob pointed at Sharon.

"Sexual harassment," she answered without hesitation.

"OK," Bob acknowledged. "What about the law firm before coming here?"

"That was where it happened, the sexual harassment."

"I thought you said money and being a 'Director' were the issues," Bob questioned.

"Well, those were certainly nice, but one of the partners kept chasing me around the desk, and I got tired of it. So here I am. I left my only other job so I could pursue law school."

Bob moved clockwise around the circle, now pointing at Lloyd.

Lloyd answered quickly. "I, too, left a job for school. In fact, I've held many part-time jobs to support my education. I've only left two permanent jobs, though, mostly because I felt I didn't fit. In each case, my style differed from the boss's. I wanted to develop meaningful relationships with clients and contribute to their growth. My bosses wanted me to make more calls and get to the bottom line more quickly. I just couldn't operate that way, so I left."

Terry spoke last. "Well, I've never left a job. This job has provided me plenty of variety and opportunity. I obviously have friends who left their companies though. Sometimes I could see leaving for the reasons they gave. For instance, one woman simply couldn't communicate with her boss and the problem was reflected as solely her fault on performance reviews — big surprise. Another friend became a mom and wanted to work less. She found a qualified person to job share, but the company wouldn't hear of it. So she became a full-time mom and left the company altogether."

Bob chimed in to share his reasons. "I've left several start-up companies. Even after being a solid contributor and helping the company get started, I was never significantly recognized for my contributions or leadership. The founders or venture capitalists often looked for the best way to get the stock price up quickly, not necessarily for the best way to assure the longevity of the product line where my team members and I worked. They would offer shallow compliments about our work, then lay out the plan for me to perform another miracle. Sometimes I even profited from their strategy. But those dollars didn't make up for how unbearable it was to announce to the group we were being sold or cut altogether."

Bob still had the floor and wanted to share what he was learning. "I think it's important for us to realize that what we say we need, while valid, doesn't hold a candle to what we absolutely must have. Let me explain. This morning my wife asked me, 'Why I Work.' We all answered her question just now. In our answers, we cited some extrinsic and intrinsic needs. Extrinsic needs are things like pay, benefits, appropriate work assignments, policies and procedures, etc. We allow other people to control them for us. While very important, extrinsic needs don't always define what we absolutely must have to stay in a job. Lloyd even said earlier he could find his extrinsic needs fulfilled elsewhere.

"What seems to be more important is the satisfaction of our intrinsic needs — the answers to 'Why I Left.' What we absolutely must have, or we'll leave. Like the things we've said: avoiding sexual harassment, seeking continuing education, valuing the client above quotas, job sharing, making a commitment to the team members. We've all felt so strongly about these intrinsic issues that we've actually left jobs to fulfill those values elsewhere! Isn't that astonishing?" He was surprised that Jessica's questions were so hard-hitting for each of them, not just himself.

Bob pulled out his personal organizer again and felt foolish doing so. He made a joke to cover by saying, "Talk amongst yourselves, today's subject…what does the Pope look like in shorts?" Bob quickly scribbled some more notes.

Why I Work	Why I Left
People may list all sorts of overt reasons for working	The bottom line needs which must be met if an individual is to remain at the company
(Both extrinsic and intrinsic needs)	(Only intrinsic needs)

Extrinsic Needs – Needs the individual allows others to fulfill and hence control.

Intrinsic Needs – Needs the individual controls and must meet, to the extent he/she will change environments in order to do so.

Terry strained to glimpse Bob's notes.

"What are you writing, Bob?" she asked.

"I've been trying to answer some questions for Jessica. I don't know exactly how they fit together yet, but we just hit part of it. Can I let you know more when I figure it out?" Bob asked.

"Well, now I'm dying of curiosity," Terry smiled as she spoke. "But if this has something to do with Jessica, I approve and will stay out of it."

Bob was visibly relieved and somewhat embarrassed. He needed a quick change of subject. Noticing the empty drink glasses, Bob suggested dinner at a nearby restaurant, the same one he dragged them to each time he was in Des Moines. They agreed and stood to leave. The bartenders jumped on the bar and began to play. What a place!

CHAPTER **8**

Answering
the Challenge

D INNER HAD BEEN FANTASTIC — GOOD FOOD AND GOOD
friends. Even so, Bob had been anxious to get
back to his room to continue working on "Jessica's
Challenge."

Over dinner, he had recognized that the "Why I Left"
and "Why I Work" questions fit perfectly into the "six boxes"
diagram — on the side of the *individual*. Bob pulled out his
shared vision diagram to add the questions.

The dinner group had determined that the answers to
"Why I Left" would reveal the failure to meet intrinsic needs.
Such a failure could be prevented. Bob realized that taking
the time to define *personal values* would allow individuals
to proactively know whether their intrinsic needs will be

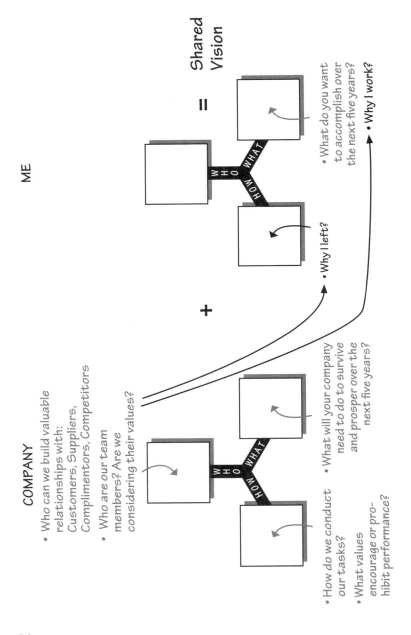

ME

COMPANY

• Who can we build valuable relationships with: Customers, Suppliers, Complimentors, Competitors

• Who are our team members? Are we considering their values?

• How do we conduct our tasks?

• What values encourage or prohibit performance?

• What will your company need to do to survive and prosper over the next five years?

WHO

WHAT

HOW

=

Shared Vision

+

• Why I left?

• What do you want to accomplish over the next five years?

• Why I work?

fulfilled at work. Certainly people leave a company when it can't satisfy psychological or physical needs. If they could "see it coming," then the team could take action to right the wrong before it happened. Knowing the *values* behind the question "Why I Left," therefore, appropriately answers the *individual's* quest for *how.*

Bob added the question below the *how* box under "Me" on his shared vision diagram.

He also recognized from his conversation with the group that "Why I Work" solicited both extrinsic and intrinsic *needs* as answers from the individual. These needs must be fulfilled, and should be represented on the diagram. The answers to this question, then, stipulated *what* the individual must do.

Bob moved to the *what* block under "Me" on his shared vision diagram and wrote "Why I Work."

The two questions made sense from all angles. If the company considered the satisfaction of each employee's mission as necessary to prevent attrition, then everyone's *values* and *needs* would have an important place in the shared vision diagram. Likewise, once the individual recognized his or her needs and values being upheld, they would invest themselves in the success of the company.

In addition, as a supervisor, Bob figured he could prevent crossing those "lines in the sand" by knowing why people left previous jobs. Bob wanted to review each team member's *who, what,* and *how.* Certainly if he knew his employees' values, he could honor them. Equally important was knowing why people wanted to work — their needs. If Bob didn't seek to satisfy *what* people were overtly looking for in their work, he would lose them just as fast. The trick was to get them to want to discover and share their intrinsic needs and values.

Bob had had enough theorizing. He took the leap and began to fill in his "ME" boxes to arrive at some semblance of a personal mission.

He started with his *who*. "Who do I serve?" This question was obviously missing, so he wrote it in. Well, he thought, I serve Jessica, Emma, and Michael. That was easy. They certainly made up a majority of his time away from work. Speaking of work, perhaps he should consider his coworkers. He certainly served his project team by contributing as an engineer and leader. He wrote in "team members and R & D group for Chip Tronix."

Now virtually all of his time was accounted for. Bob strained to consider if he served others in his life. "On Mondays, I volunteer as a tutor for students studying for their GEDs. So the *who* in that case would be the teachers and students. I coach little league in the spring. So the *who* there would be the players and their parents. I serve as a reader at church, so the *who* would be the church community." He chuckled with a realization. "Boy, I sure spend a lot of time helping just a few people," he thought sarcastically.

"Well, I've already answered 'Why I Left,' so let me just fill those in." Bob began transcribing his answers from the cocktail meeting to the page. He reflected on the importance of his contribution to the team. If he and his team members weren't allowed to right the ship, then it wasn't worth staying on. It didn't look like much on paper, but he felt he'd been put on Earth to help others reach their potential. If he couldn't do that, he'd look elsewhere for work. Finally, he added "Receiving recognition for being a contributor." He remembered the shallow compliments at the "start ups" where he once worked. The lack of recognition caused him to leave those companies.

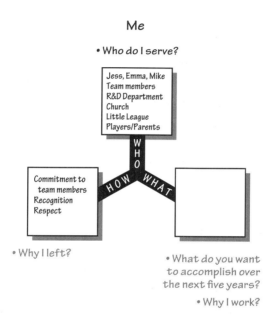

Now, the hard questions. "What do I want to do over the next five years and why do I work?"

Why he worked was a necessity now, not a choice. What he did over the next five years seemed predetermined. Even more preposterous was to consider who to work for and why. He hadn't done that since he finished college.

"What do I want to do over the next five years?" Being with Jessica and the children was at the core of that answer.

Bob wrote down his answers in the box. (1) Raise children and support them in their activities and growth. That was number one on his list even though it didn't seem to get number one treatment. He also felt strongly about (2) helping Jessica go back to school to get her MBA. Studying with her would allow him to learn about the latest trends and theories, and (3) improve his professional skills. To that end, he probably should attend a seminar or two a year concerning his technical field. In five years, it would also be time to (4) move up to a director-level position. His project management experience would be quite extensive at that point, certainly enough to serve him as the director of R & D somewhere. Finally, he had always wanted to (5) travel to Australia and Asia. "Might as well throw Scandinavia in there as long as we're dreamin'," he joked.

He moved on to the question, "Why I Work." Bob was surprised at how easily his pen inked answers to this question. He wanted to (6) help others achieve their unrealized potential in the work place, (7) use science to create products that help the world, and (8) provide support and benefits for the family.

He was astonished he had never taken the time to write down "his" mission. It didn't take very long. After all, it was "his" mission. He didn't have to endure the "wordsmithing" phase of a corporate mission statement session. What he wrote down was exactly what he wanted to be.

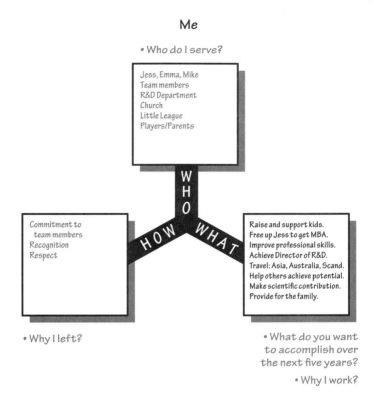

Me

• Who do I serve?

Jess, Emma, Mike
Team members
R&D Department
Church
Little League
Players/Parents

WHO

HOW

WHAT

Commitment to
  team members
Recognition
Respect

Raise and support kids.
Free up Jess to get MBA.
Improve professional skills.
Achieve Director of R&D.
Travel: Asia, Australia, Scand.
Help others achieve potential.
Make scientific contribution.
Provide for the family.

• Why I left?

• What do you want
  to accomplish over
  the next five years?
  • Why I work?

Bob knew writing the company's mission would be just as revealing, but he was running out of steam. It had been a long day. He piled the pillows against the headboard of the bed and watched TV. No interruptions or disputes over the remote — just recuperation time. It was good to be king.

CHAPTER **9**

Self-Discovery

M EETINGS IN THE HOTEL HAD ADVANTAGES. BOB COULD sleep until thirty minutes before the start, then raid the catered continental breakfast minutes before meeting time. He got more sleep on meeting days than he did at home!

Today's meeting setup was typical, with a horseshoe table, and an overhead projector and flip chart placed in the front of the room. Bob dropped his notebook at an empty seat and made a beeline for the breakfast table. All of the expected players were there. Lloyd, Terry, Sharon, Bob's boss Ramin, Todd, and four others from headquarters. Bob was the lone "outsider" at the meeting. A woman in her late 30s was speaking with Todd. Bob didn't recognize her. He had more immediate issues on his mind: bear claws.

Todd, the CEO, started the meeting in his usual outspoken way. "OK, everyone, let's get started." The crowd quietly settled down. "As you know, I've called this meeting to discuss our corporate direction. You may feel we've already determined our direction, in no uncertain terms, by virtue of the budget decisions we announced earlier this week. Those cuts were aimed at our structure, and are going to have some effect on our long-term direction. With that said, however, I believe the future of this company can be determined right here in this room." Todd was very good at making eye contact with his audience. He made each person feel as if he was talking directly to him or her. Todd moved in and out of the horseshoe and circled the podium, keeping everyone at ease with his casual movement. "With such a large amount at stake, I don't want this meeting to get off on the wrong foot. That is, I don't want folks to bite each other's heads off. So I've hired someone to preserve the peace and help us learn a bit about ourselves."

This was a surprise, Bob thought. No empire building or budget battles? Certainly some management consultant couldn't solve their problems in a day.

"Dr. Charlotte O'Connell is from New York where I heard her speak last month at my young presidents' meeting. Her expertise is in corporate culture. All you MBAs," he said, mocking those with the degree he lacked, "know that how we interact with each other at work isn't simply a reflection of our own personalities. It's also a reflection of the character of the whole company. I was intrigued by Charlotte's suggestion that our culture — the values we use as a group in order to function — will either propel or destroy our future. So I approached her at a break, and I explained our upcoming budget cuts and the need for a culture change.

She told me I couldn't do it! I naturally tried to defend myself and informed her that, as CEO, I most certainly could do it! She immediately replied that the only group I might influence…" Todd slowed his speech to emphasize his words, "was the small group that was structurally below me — this group here today. In this group, I could use my influence in one of two ways. I could control people and pursue *my* direction, or I could develop your trust and pursue a *shared* direction. Charlotte made it clear that I could only lead when you entrusted me with the power to lead. If you didn't trust me, I wasn't leading you anywhere. Autocracy or leadership: it was my choice.

"I wasn't sold, until after I heard her presentation on *self-discovery* of our 'true' personality type. Understanding this process of self-discovery made it clear what I had to do. I hope you'll arrive at similar conclusions after seeing her presentation. Rather than steal any more of her thunder, I'll turn it over to Charlotte."

Charlotte silently flipped on an overhead projector, revealing a simple slide.

Adapted with permission from *Temperament and Type Dynamics, the Facilitator's Guide* (Telos Publications, CA. 1995).

"What are these?" she asked.

"Manhole covers, saucers, disks," came various answers from the group.

Charlotte pulled out another slide.

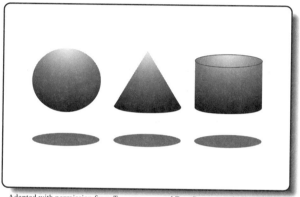

Adapted with permission from *Temperament and Type Dynamics, the Facilitator's Guide* (Telos Publications, CA. 1995).

"What now?"

Chuckles from the group answered her question.

"When looking at another's personality, we tend to judge the entire object by the shadow, or the behavior, we see. Yet, the object behind the shadow may be completely different than our impression led us to believe. Likewise, in a different situation, we may see an altogether different shadow of the same object, or person." She put up a new slide.

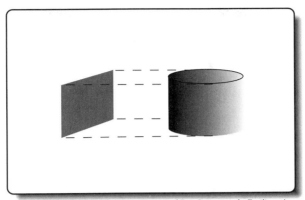

Adapted with permission from *Temperament and Type Dynamics, the Facilitator's Guide* (Telos Publications, CA. 1995).

"When we work with someone new, we initially see many different shadows depending on the situation. A different situation, a different shadow. As observers of shadows, we actually get pretty good at anticipating what kind of shadow we're going to see from a person in a given situation, don't we? So we tend to filter information. We try to predict the shadows we'll see."

Charlotte posed a question to the group, "Who owns the filter that helps us predict shadows, or behavior?"

"We do," someone offered.

"That's correct. You do. I do. Each of us has a filter or an array of filters that vary with the situation. What are our filters comprised of?"

"They are who we are," Lloyd volunteered. "Our filters are a collection of our life's experiences and the feelings we have about those experiences."

"Excellent." Charlotte smiled. "And another way of saying

our life's experiences and feelings is — our personalities. Each of us has a unique personality. An array of likes and dislikes, preferences, decision processes, and behaviors. Each of us is unique. Our life's experiences are unique. We may share a viewpoint with some folks in one area, then have differing viewpoints in other areas. We are unique.

"Today we're going to examine what causes our viewpoints to be alike or dissimilar. We'll use several personality and temperament models to determine the unique values and needs that drive our personal behavior. After all, our core values and needs tell us what we like and dislike, what we prefer, how to make a decision, and how to act. They are at the core of our personalities. Sometimes we share them with others. Sometimes we do not and disagree passionately.

"I've found that using only one personality preference indicator often leads to erroneous findings. We tend to select who we *want* to be, and not who we are. So I've started using many different models, both objective and subjective, to help us get to our 'best fit.' The first model we'll use is David Keirsey's four temperaments, then we'll examine the characteristics of the those temperaments. We'll also look at the work of Carl Jung, who described the different ways of perceiving and judging information. Finally, we'll wrap up with the Myers-Briggs Type Indicator®. Remember, none of these will necessarily be a definitive representation of *who* you are. We'll need to get many points of view to avoid being inaccurate. Only by honestly reviewing the separate qualities of the temperaments and mental processes can you arrive at your true perspective. In fact, that's our goal for today: to find your 'true' personality type.

"Your 'true' personality type, who you truly are, is driven by those core values and needs I mentioned. I know it's hard to believe," she said jokingly, "but most of us differ when it comes to these core issues.

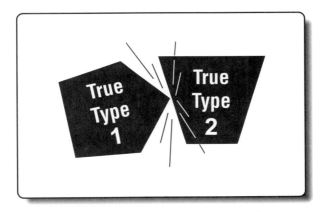

"Unfortunately, when you deal with people who have different values and needs, conflict can easily erupt. So over time, we start to develop adaptive behavior. Adaptive behavior doesn't naturally reflect our true desires in the short term, but allows us to 'fake it' enough to get along with others.

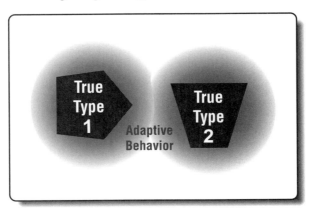

After several decades of using adaptive behavior in our various roles — parent, employee, employer, soccer coach, parishioner, etc. — most of us begin to lose sight of what we originally valued or needed. This suppression has consequences. In fact, I've had several people in class discover the real reasons why they left their jobs after years of hiding behind adaptive behavior. They are usually quite shocked to learn they were seeking their core values in those jobs and were unable to find them — so they had no choice but to leave. When they quit, they thought they just 'didn't fit' or were simply 'unable to stay.' But in reality, it was only a matter of time before they sought out their core psychological needs elsewhere.

"So we're left with a paradox. We can't survive without adaptive behavior creating harmony. But when we can't see how our values will be met in a relationship (such as with your boss), we may appear to the other person as being inauthentic or uninterested — destroying trust and the relationship — forcing a drastic change."

"I'm not sure how I would appear inauthentic," Lloyd interrupted.

Charlotte considered his question and then responded. "Let's say I determine that my core need is to have empathic relationships. At work, I'm a supervisor and a big budget cut forces me to lay off three workers. Now, laying people off doesn't allow me to achieve my value. I'm naturally empathic to their situation. Yet I have to stand firm for the company because I don't want the other workers to panic. How effective do you think I'm going to be at representing the company when

I tell these three people they are laid off? If I take a hard-line approach, I'll definitely appear to be inauthentic. They already know me as a 'people person.'"

"You know, I've had to do that exact thing and felt extremely uncomfortable. Now I know why," Lloyd confessed.

Charlotte smiled and nodded at Lloyd's realization. "Today, therefore, it's imperative for us to learn what our true values and needs are. If you can define your individual preferences and share them with your fellow employees, then we can both understand your direction as an individual and build a shared direction as a group. In fact, this 'values and needs' perspective will give you a new outlook on how to communicate better, how to empower people with goals matched to their strengths, and how to keep the peace on group direction. When you know your true core needs, you can be honest about their satisfaction and implore others to be forthright in satisfying what's important to them. People worry about how to improve motivation and morale. Well, this is it. Together we can get to that illusive, best-possible solution."

Bob was shocked that Charlotte's conclusion was the same thing Jessica had said in the car. Only when an individual knew his or her core values and needs would be satisfied by the group could he or she take responsibility for the group's failure or success. Likewise, the group needed to plan on using the differing perspectives of its members to consistently achieve the best possible solutions.

"Now, to address the temperaments, I'd like to use some animal metaphors to get us going." Charlotte put up a slide of a fox. "What do you know about the fox?" Charlotte went to a flip chart and titled it 'fox.'

Members of the group yelled out answers: "cunning . . . fast . . . opportunistic . . . tactical . . . alert . . . skilled . . . partnering." Charlotte wrote on the flip chart as fast as she could. Then she put up a slide showing the needs and values of the Artisan temperament.

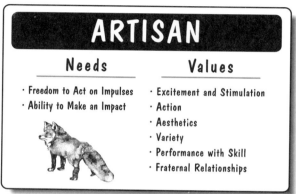

Adapted with permission from Linda V. Berens, *Understanding Yourself and Others, An Introduction to Temperament* (Telos Publications, CA. 1998).

"The fox is a metaphor for the Artisan temperament. Like foxes, Artisans need to know they have the freedom to respond to the needs of the moment. Telling Artisans you appreciate their input but you'll be handling the decisions on the account is like telling a kid at Disneyland she can't ride any of the rides. Not only do Artisans want the freedom to contribute in whatever way makes sense to them, they must have your feedback on how they singularly impacted the job or task. They need to know that they 'made it happen' or where they failed.

"Artisans have a unique perspective that may be keenly needed by your company, don't they? And guess what will happen if you, or someone in your group, doesn't provide for their needs?"

"They're hittin' the road," Terry stepped in.

"That's right. Certainly pay and benefits need to be met at some minimum level, but most people don't leave jobs because of pay. In your industry, for instance, pay, benefits, and stock options aren't too terribly different among the major competitors, are they? So why would employees leave their jobs to go to a competitor with the same offering?" She asked the question rhetorically, then rephrased it. "Who here has left a well-paying job with benefits?"

Everyone except Terry raised a hand.

"Why?" Charlotte pursued her audience.

"Poor communication with the boss . . . not respected for my ideas or capacity to grow . . . not recognized for significant contributions to the company . . . sexual harassment." The input came from all corners of the room.

"So just in our small group here, we're beginning to see our core values have a major place at work." She stopped to let them reflect on what they had just heard.

"Let's move on to the second temperament." Charlotte continued with the same approach for each temperament, using a beaver for the Guardian temperament, an owl for the Rational, and a dolphin for the Idealist.

GUARDIAN

Needs	Values
• Membership or Belonging	• Group/Bonding Relationships
• Responsibility or Duty	• Stability
	• Hierarchical Procedures
	• Security
	• Conformity
	• Preservation of Social Groups
	• Rules and Regulations

Adapted with permission from Linda V. Berens, *Understanding Yourself and Others, An Introduction to Temperament* (Telos Publications, CA. 1998).

Bob couldn't believe his eyes. He was seeing a version of the *Real Life* magazine article and it was making sense! Guardians have to have the group succeed. In fact, they have a duty to ensure that it does. Guardians need to know the plan for the project, the budget, promotion, continuing education, everything. More importantly, they need to know how they fit into the plan.

Rationals have to completely understand the concept at hand and master it. They could spend hours overcoming a problem that intrigued them. If they couldn't solve it, they would have to at least understand the situation completely. Usually strategically oriented, Rationals are skilled at inventing, designing, and defining in their quest for achievement.

RATIONAL

Needs	Values
• Mastery and Self Control	• Expert Relationships
• Knowledge and Competence	• Logical Consistency
	• Scientific Inquiry
	• Intelligence
	• Ultimate Truths or Theories
	• Progress
	• Concepts and Ideas

Adapted with permission from Linda V. Berens, *Understanding Yourself and Others, An Introduction to Temperament* (Telos Publications, CA. 1998).

Idealists are dead in the water without meaningful relationships. They seek them out to better understand their personal purpose on the planet. Idealists are gifted with intuition and imagination in their quest for fostering and facilitating meaningful growth among their communities. The Idealist seeks unity by promoting authentic and moral behavior. To deny an Idealist a meaningful relationship over the long haul would be worse than withholding the year-end bonus check.

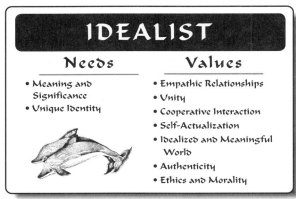

IDEALIST

Needs	Values
• Meaning and Significance	• Empathic Relationships
• Unique Identity	• Unity
	• Cooperative Interaction
	• Self-Actualization
	• Idealized and Meaningful World
	• Authenticity
	• Ethics and Morality

Adapted with permission from Linda V. Berens, *Understanding Yourself and Others, An Introduction to Temperament* (Telos Publications, CA. 1998).

In fact, to deny anyone of his or her core needs in the long term means one thing — those needs will be satisfied elsewhere. The unique needs and values are, in the end, why they came to work. They have to be satisfied every day.

Charlotte took the group through a battery of exercises to show how each person perceives and then judges information. She even distributed the results of the Myers-Briggs Type Indicator®. It was gradually becoming apparent to Bob that he was a Guardian. Charlotte emphasized throughout the morning that each framework was only a lens or data point, and each person should wait until the end of the entire process to find his or her best fit. Bob, in fact, found that he shared many values with the other temperaments, but his core needs created an undeniable fire within him that had to be quenched. Those needs matched with the Guardian characteristics. Taking care of the family, providing a stable and secure home, keeping people together, helping others succeed, enforcing company policies, seeking out rules and regulations in unclear situations. This described Bob — right to the core.

Toward the end of the morning, everyone in the group began to discover truths about themselves. Charlotte announced that disclosing their "true" personality type was strictly voluntary. However, everyone was so excited about their discoveries that sharing became a natural outcome. Lloyd an Idealist, Terry and Todd, Artisans, Sharon and Ramin, Rationals.

Exercises done throughout the day had shown each person's differing viewpoints and perspectives. What Bob perceived as "conflict" during the exercises, he could now see as viewpoints clearly aligned with values defined by the temperaments. For instance, in a mock budget cut exercise, Lloyd, the Idealist, wanted everyone to emphasize the human factor of lost intellectual capital caused by the pretend cuts. Ramin and Sharon, the Rationals, strategically looked at saving money and new ways of creating revenue so that the company could survive, helping more people in the long run.

What was seemingly a deep-rooted conflict could now be viewed as simply a two-temperament look at the same problem. Surprisingly, Todd, the Artisan, wasn't threatened by the diverse viewpoints. He welcomed them! He wanted their knowledge so that he could make the best decisions concerning so many people.

As a result, Bob saw that the best solution did not come from a single temperament or the "group think" that results from a group made up of the same temperament. The best possible solution would come from a group made up of all the temperaments. Each temperament possessed unique values that offered valid and vital components for both the employee's and the company's long-term survival and profitability. Members of a group made up of the same temperament would be blind to many perspectives that could potentially harm them; likewise, possible solutions to their problems might be invisible to such a homogenous group.

To Bob, then, Step 1 in working together and being productive should be to know the temperaments of your people and include all types in problem solving. Step 2 should be, if you don't have all the temperaments represented in your group, either get them or seek their input! Bob made an annotation on his notepad.

> The best possible solution consistently comes from a group in which members from all four temperaments are included in problem solving and process improvement.

PART

BALANCING
VALUES

CHAPTER **10**

Achieving
Shared Vision

C HARLOTTE CONCLUDED THE FORMAL SELF-DISCOVERY process at 5 p.m. However, the group could sense there was more to learn. Just about everyone agreed to adjourn to the bar.

The bartenders had just finished a jazz set. Terry and Bob pulled two tables together for the group. Sharon summoned a waiter to bring the coveted popcorn. Todd, Ramin, and Lloyd delivered everyone's coats to the coat rack on the side of the bar.

"Well, I never would have guessed we'd spend the first day of this seminar learning about ourselves, but I enjoyed it. I hope we're able to tie all this into Todd's master plan: 'the future of the company is in this room.'" Lloyd ribbed Todd simply because he could.

"I think we'll be able to," Todd candidly responded. "When I first heard Charlotte speak last month, her ideas bowled me over. I couldn't believe my perception of a problem could possibly be different from yours simply because of a 'core value.'" Todd spit out the words, demonstrating his initial reluctance at accepting the concept. "I had always believed it was only our position and role in the company that motivated our inputs. I would think to myself, the accountant is just saying such and such because she's the accountant. Her argument must be based on her perspective as an accountant — not because of who she is as a person. As you can see, I had a limited understanding of our personality diversity. Charlotte's revelation was quite important for me.

"Knowing the importance of this meeting, I thought having her speak would help us understand how to use our different perspectives more fully in our planning. I wish Charlotte could have stayed another day. The real work begins tomorrow with the planning.

"I found today's seminar astounding as well," Sharon added. "In fact, it fit in with what we talked about last night. A question was posed, 'Why Do We Work?' When we tried to answer the question, we all expressed quite different needs and values — just like in the seminar today. Last night, I found I sometimes shared needs and values with others, which is only natural. But today I felt 'set free' when I learned about *my* core values and needs. I agree with Charlotte. Undeniably those needs must be met in my life, and especially in my professional life. Until today, I wouldn't have thought this important personal information could be revealed in such an unintrusive way."

Bob piped up. "You know, I think there is a way to tie this all together."

"Oh, really, Guardian Boy. How so?" Terry asked.

"Well, as some of you remember, my wife Jessica challenged me on these very issues on our drive to the airport yesterday. She got on a roll as only Jessica can do. However, she came up with some solid ideas that tie right into what we're doing. If you don't mind, let's try her idea and see if it works. We might get to tomorrow's bottom line tonight." Bob offered the idea somewhat reluctantly, as it had already been a long day.

He scanned the group for dissenters, but everyone okayed his quest. The drinks and popcorn arrived, and they began to relax.

Bob went to the bar and grabbed a wad of cocktail napkins. He dealt six napkins to each person. "Does everyone have a pen?" A few exchanges took place while Bob continued. "Okay, now number your napkins on the top left side, one through six." While they numbered the napkins, Bob pulled out his personal organizer and quickly flipped to his notes.

"I'm going to ask you six questions. Answer each question on each of the six napkins. Here's the first question: 'Why do you work?' You can write that on top of your napkin if you'd like." He repeated the question for those still writing. "Why do you work? Now that's a big question, so it may be easier to answer something more specific like — what do you want to accomplish over the next five years?" The group took several minutes answering each of Bob's questions:

1. Why do you work? What do you want to accomplish over the next five years?
2. Who do you serve in your life?
3. Why have you left jobs or groups before?
4. What will our group need to do to survive and prosper over the next five years?
5. What values in the workplace enhance or encourage performance? How do we conduct tasks?
6. Who can our group build/maintain valuable relationships with?

Before long, everyone had several napkin lists.

"Now go back to your napkins and pick out the two most important items on each one. Circle them, or cross the others out, to distinguish your answers. Be sure to look for your core needs and values within each item. Remember, the needs and values of the temperaments manifest themselves in our lives in unique ways. Look for those ways in your answers. For example, as a Guardian, my personal success is tied directly to the success of my R & D group.

"You may notice a core need or value missing in your answers. Identify that need or value as missing and circle it as well."

Bob started to get a bit nervous. This might turn out to be a bust. He was betting on Jessica though. This must be how she got everyone to love her. She sought shared vision.

Bob quickly copied his notes from the night before to some napkins.

"Let me explain what we're doing here. Charlotte said the only way Todd, or any of us, could lead a small group was to establish trust. We would have to trust Todd and give him the power to lead us. Otherwise we'd be hitting the road, as Lloyd said — right? And the only way to trust each other would logically be if we believed Todd was doing his best for both the group and us. So what, then, is best for us and the group?" Bob pulled out his chart of shared vision and pointed at the company's three boxes.

"Well, in business school," he smiled at Todd to return the jab given earlier in the day, "we learned it's best for a company to do its mission. A mission is comprised of who, what, and how."

"Yeah, yeah, yeah, we spent an entire semester on mission statements in organizational behavior class," Terry rolled her eyes as she spoke. "Don't tell me these napkins are another way of doing the company mission statement?" She hoped for relief from something she had done many times before with futile results.

"Well, in part, yes. The company has to do its job. As employees, we make sure that job gets done. Periodically, we also have to redefine what the job is and who it's done for. You know, the process improvement and quality stuff we do." Bob paused long enough to point his pen at the individual's three boxes. "But just as we have a responsibility to help the company do its thing, the group has a responsibility to help its employees do theirs. When we perform both missions together, the needs and values of the group are met ... and the needs and values of the employee are met! We arrive at a truly shared vision. In fact, this model could be used for any group in our company."

"So in this model, the company has a responsibility to make

sure I spend adequate time with my sons?" Ramin questioned.

"That's right. If you've determined that spending time with your sons 'feeds' a core need, as Charlotte said today, the company has as much responsibility for making sure you're out the door at 5 P.M. as you have for making sure the production line stays operational. It's a win/win proposition. If the company provides for you by meeting and using your core needs, you'll most likely stick around for a long time — gracing us with your presence. Likewise, you'll be more motivated to ensure the production line stays up and running so that the company can survive and prosper. After all, your perspective, as a Rational, is being used to define the group's success."

"It's a two-way street," Lloyd added. "I'll scratch your back, you scratch mine."

"You're right, but it's even more than that. Remember how we learned from Charlotte that the best possible solution could only occur when all four temperaments contributed to finding it?"

"Yes," Lloyd answered.

"So when we all say what we think the company should do over the next five years, what we're really creating is a four-temperament look at what's important for the company. The group gets the benefit of our diversity in defining its direction — limiting blind spots and creating collaborative solutions. The result is a shared vision of the best possible solution."

The group was clearly interested in Bob's diagram and the shared vision idea, but he could see that he hadn't connected with everyone yet.

"Enough of the philosophy. Let's try this and see if it makes sense." Bob was eager to get everyone in the group on board.

"Okay, everyone find napkin number 1 and put it on the table." Bob took care to assemble the napkins equally. Many of them had written down similar values.

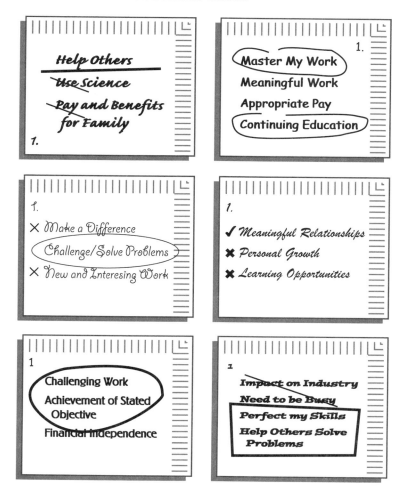

Bob tore out a large blank piece of paper and put it in the center of the cocktail table. He quickly drew his diagram of the six boxes of shared vision. Bob began to fill in the first box with each napkin's top two values or needs.

Terry spoke out, "I get it. Here let me do this." Terry took her pen and began to fill in the boxes for Bob. She finished the first box and had everyone put out the second set of napkins. Then she filled in the second box. Before long, Bob's diagram was completed.

While they worked, Bob struggled to find the hub that would hold the spokes of this wheel together. Shared vision needed to include answers from all six questions. But which answers? All of them were important. After all, both the company and the employee needed to win. The answers would not only define what the company needed to do to survive, they would also spell out what the *individuals* needed to do to survive. *Both* were of equal importance. Therefore, their mission would be to do all, or at least most, of the answers on the napkins.

Then he saw it. The "six box" diagram was actually a map ... a map that would show them where to go. They didn't have to include everything on their trip, but they could see what *must* be done for the group and its members to prosper.

Everyone was excited about completing the six boxes. Each could see his or her contribution as vital.

"Great," Sharon said. "This is how you pull it all together. Now we can see what needs to happen for our small group. Granted it's only a part of Chip Tronix, but certainly the most important part to me. As a lawyer, though," she retreated

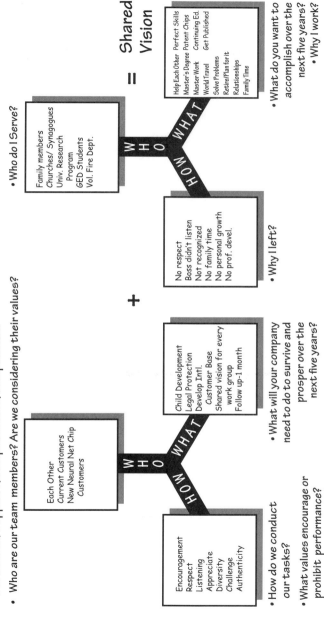

ME

- Who do I Serve?

Who do I Serve?
Family members
Churches/ Synagogues
Univ. Research
Program
GED Students
Vol. Fire Dept.

WHO / WHAT / HOW

What (what do you want to accomplish)
Help Each Other Perfect Skills
Master's Degree Patent Chips
Master Work Continuing Ed.
World Travel Get Published
Solve Problems
Retire/Plan for it
Relationships
Family Time

- What do you want to accomplish over the next five years?
- Why I work?

Why I left?
No respect
Boss didn't listen
Not recognized
No family time
No personal growth
No prof. devel.

- Why I left?

Shared Vision

=

+

COMPANY

- Who can we build valuable relationships with: Customers, Suppliers, Complimentors, Competition.
- Who are our team members? Are we considering their values?

Who
Each Other
Current Customers
New Neural Net Chip
Customers

WHO / WHAT / HOW

What
Child Development
Legal Protection
Develop Intl.
Customer Base
Shared vision for every work group
Follow up-1 month

- What will your company need to do to survive and prosper over the next five years?

How
Encouragement
Respect
Listening
Appreciate
Diversity
Challenge
Authenticity

- How do we conduct our tasks?
- What values encourage or prohibit performance?

pessimistically, "I know how it goes from here. Everyone says these are super ideas and two days from now, they are the furthest things from anyone's mind. We need a contract to hold ourselves to this."

"Excellent idea!" Todd exclaimed, excited about the progress the group was making.

"Bob, can I have another blank sheet of paper?" Sharon asked. Bob tore out a page and passed it to her. Sharon began to write, organizing her thoughts into sentences of intent. She wrote one sentence for the content of each of the boxes. She worked quickly and accurately; it was easy to understand why she was successful in the courtroom.

Sharon presented her "contract" to the group.

Contract for Shared Vision

We recognize why we belong to this team: _____

_____

_____ and _____

_____

(Why I Work)

We also recognize in order to retain our team members we must
promote_____

_____ and _____

(Why I Left)

We will support our team members' _____

_____ and _____

_____

(What Do You Want to Accomplish in the Next 5 Years?)

goal accomplishment by upholding these values:

_____

_____ and —————

_____

(What Values in the Workplace Enhance or Encourage Performance?)

We will ensure our group/company's survival or prosperity by
tackling these issues: _____

_____

_____

_____ and _____

_____

(What Will Your Group Need to Do to Survive and Prosper over the Next 5 Years?)

So that our team members can serve:

_____

(Who Do I Serve?)

We recognize the following relationships as containing
tangible worth for our group/company to improve/pursue:

_____ and _____

(Who Can Our Group Maintain Valuable Relationships with?)

"Now all we have to do is fill it in," Terry suggested.

Sharon was pleased that Terry saw the value of her idea and passed the contract to her. Sharon knew Terry would get everyone to buy into its validity. Terry transferred the data from the six boxes to the contract.

After writing the first paragraph, Terry had everyone help her fill in the remaining lines. They looked for similarities and wrote them in first. Then, she entertained the ideas that everyone felt most strongly about. It wasn't hard. Several times people jumped on the idea of another, saying they wished they had thought of it.

They soon completed their description of shared vision.

There it was. A "Shared Vision" for their group. No trainer was telling them to brainstorm what was most important to the company. The napkins told the story. Everything was literally on the table, at least for this group. The self-discovery they had done with Charlotte made it okay to be different, and the napkins simply reflected that uniqueness. Sometimes their values and needs overlapped, sometimes they didn't. The vision statement simply made them all equally important. If "the future of the company was in that room" as Todd had stated, then the requirements of their shared vision now lay before them.

"Well, the last time I tried to write a mission statement for the company, it took three days and we still had to compromise at the end," Todd said. "Now we've come up with a collaborative vision for our group in just forty-five minutes. One that everyone's happy with! I guess we wasted money on that mission statement guy last year," he laughed.

Contract for Shared Vision

We recognize why we belong to this team: to help each other, master our work, solve challenging problems, promote meaningful relationships, and perfect our skills through continuing education.

We also recognize in order to retain our team members we must promote *personal growth*, *enforce mutual respect*, *listen to subordinates*, *recognize contributions*, and *enforce family time*.

We will support our team members' *continuing education, travel, retirement, preparation, family time,* and *skill development*
goal accomplishment by upholding these values: *encouragement, respect, listening, appreciating, diversity, welcoming growth opportunities,* and *being authentic.*

We will ensure our group/company's survival or prosperity by tackling these issues: **neural net chip development, legally protecting our inventions, develop an international customer base for the neural net chip,** and **formal follow-up on this vision in six months.**

So that our team members can serve: **their families and communities.**

We recognize the following relationships as containing tangible worth for our group/company to improve/pursue: *each other, prospective clients,* and *current customers.*

Everyone began to smile. Each of them realized they were all needed to define the group's success. Everyone had a stake, an expected result, and a responsibility to hold each other to task. Todd didn't determine the direction—they all did. Pleasing the boss was no longer the primary motivation; pleasing the group was now a responsibility.

Todd continued, "If every group in our company did this, then we'd have a great idea of what our company's culture really is. We'd also get some clarity as to where we should be heading. I bet seeing all our work groups' visions together could tell us if our strategic plan can work.

"Next, I suggest we create an action plan to make our group's contract work. Of course, we may have to make some policy or structural changes to support the vision," Todd conjectured. "But we now know what to base those changes on. Tomorrow, we just have to come up with short- and long-term goals for accomplishing the contract. Come to think of it, now it'll probably be even easier to get you to take responsibility for the accomplishment of these goals. We're all passionately tied to at least one or two of the items."

Lloyd was elated. He especially liked how Todd and Ramin, previously social outsiders, had come into the fold. "You know, every organization I've worked for has had a mission statement, usually composed by someone who felt passionately about the direction of the company," Lloyd said.

"At all of my previous companies, that would have been the president," Ramin suggested sarcastically.

"Yes, or the designated draftee," Lloyd added. "And that

mission statement was usually presented at the stockholder meeting, and maybe a few mandatory company meetings. But it wasn't really used, nor was it functional. Now, we have a functional vision of what we could be — which we've all contributed to. I've never been at a company whose leaders said what they were going to do, then committed to it." Lloyd tempered his optimism with caution. "I have confidence that this group is committed to our contract. But when I go back to my marketing group and do this with them, what if someone doesn't want to participate in that group's shared vision?" Lloyd asked hypothetically.

"That's just it; it's a shared vision," Bob chimed in. "People who don't share the vision won't want to stay. This is exactly why we attempted to include everyone's core needs in the development of the contract. If people aren't mature enough to appreciate how this affects them, I don't think we'll have to ask them to leave. They'll simply want to leave."

"As a supervisor, there's another part to this that I really like," Ramin added. "If a few 'bad apples' stay on, it's no longer just my responsibility to get them to do what they're supposed to do. It's now everyone's responsibility. That's why group values are so important. Those values, which we all said we needed, are now our laws. Anyone on the team can enforce these laws. The supervisor no longer has to be the 'heavy.' Now, we can compare individual behavior with the group's values, not personal standards. It's the 'bad apple' versus the group values, not the 'bad apple' versus me."

"You're right," Lloyd confirmed. "I hadn't considered that perspective, but what a great benefit. I hate being the 'heavy' as well."

Todd felt energized from the day's success. "I always knew all of you would be the future of Chip Tronix," he announced. "I'm convinced that we'll achieve this shared vision. Looks like Charlotte O'Connell earned her fee by helping us appreciate our diversity. And where's Jessica Sippel?" Todd smiled at Bob. "Get her on a plane so she can facilitate our planning session tomorrow."

"Well, it's Wednesday night — bath night. She has more pressing duties," Bob responded.

"Well then, I guess it's up to us," Todd said.

CHAPTER **11**

Achieving
Balance at Home

B OB GRABBED HIS LAST BAG FROM THE CAROUSEL AND HEADED outside. He had told Jessica to pick him up at the curb at 6:30 p.m. and it was already 6:50 p.m. He knew she would more than likely be late. Sure enough, he caught sight of the mini-van just pulling in. The rear hatch came up. His bags went in and Bob eagerly hopped into the passenger's seat. He was thrilled his entire family had decided to meet him. He greeted them with exuberance. "Hi family. You three are a majority of the 'who' and 'what' in my mission!"

"Honey, what are you talking about?"

"Sorry. I'm still a little excited, but it sure is good to see you all."

"Good to see you, Dad!" came echoing from the back.

As Jessica pulled into traffic, Bob launched into his successes. "Well, I answered your questions. I filled the boxes and finished my personal quest for vision. In fact, my aforementioned nemesis ... corporate ... " he paused to make sure she was listening, "now has an action plan for the director's group to achieve shared vision. Thanks to your Mom," he proudly announced to the kids.

Jessica smiled broadly, surprised and elated that she had made such an impact on him. It took all of her willpower to keep her eyes on the road and not hug him.

"That's great. But I thought we were going to talk about that tonight, and what did I have to do with corporate's shared vision?" asked Jessica, fishing for a compliment.

"Well, we were, but let's be spontaneous. Plus, I want the whole family to hear what I have to say."

"And the kids will understand?"

"The kids are part of it."

"Well, Bob, since you seem ready to take this on while I fight traffic, and since you say the family is part if it, and since I somehow had a hand in creating Chip Tronix's action plan, why don't I tell you what I think happened these past few days?"

Bob knew he couldn't stop her. After all, she was primarily responsible for the process. He could impress her with the details later. "Sure, Jess, give it a shot."

"Okay. You guys finally figured out the difference between a group of people working together and a team. A team not only works together, but cares as much about each other as it does about the team's actual work — which is quite a bit. A team not only performs its group mission, but it ensures each team member is able to complete his or her personal mission."

Bob wasn't surprised that her first guess was right on target.

"You were then able to put all this information into quantifiable terms. You probably used beer coasters, napkins, or something, so that each person could write down answers to the six questions you came up with from your diagram. When these napkins were displayed together, everyone could plainly see all of the raw materials comprising shared vision for your group: not for Chip Tronix in its entirety, of course, just for your group. Every other group at Chip Tronix, whether temporary or permanent, would have to conduct this exercise for themselves if they wanted to achieve shared vision."

Bob looked at her with astonishment, too stunned to interrupt.

"After all, shared vision is what motivation is all about. When people recognize it is in their best interest to act in their group's or company's best interest, then they'll do so. But the only way we can understand how our personal core needs tie to the group's core needs is to go through the *Self-Discovery Process*™ for ourselves. To learn precisely what our core needs and values are. Often they're hidden by the adaptive behavior we use in the day-to-day roles we play. So a variety of tests are needed to root out our 'true' personality type.

"Finding our 'true' personality type is important in building authentic relationships. Trust can only develop among team members when each understands the accurate needs and values of the others. Such a disclosure is so personal that it can only be made voluntarily by each team member, and should never be used as a requirement of employment."

The expression on Bob's face was changing from amazement to suspicion.

Jessica continued. "With everyone then wanting to accomplish the shared vision, you translated the data from the napkins to the 'six box' diagram. Undoubtedly, you 'Mr. Can't We All Just Get Along' probably took everyone's highest priorities and made a contract to accomplish the shared vision. With that contract in hand, the rest was easy. All you had to do was write short- and long-term goals that would satisfy the contract. A contract that, by the way, met the needs of both the group and the individuals in it. So everyone was more than willing to take on responsibility for leading the team to accomplish one or more of the goals: a natural form of empowerment.

"Todd probably concluded the meeting by saying something like: 'This stuff takes time. It doesn't happen overnight. A team can only happen through honest communication, willingness to accept failure on the way to success, and trust in each other.' Then he probably added, 'It also takes an acceptance of diversity of all kinds to get to the best possible solution. Even if Guardians have a hard time understanding just how we Artisans can be so flighty.'"

"So who called you?" Bob poised, knowing full well Jessica wasn't a psychic.

"Mr. Idealist, Lloyd, called to thank me," she confessed. "Sounds like you all might just make it." Jessica beamed with delight. "I'm very proud of you, Bob. All I had wanted you to consider was what you wanted out of work, then Lloyd tells me you got all of them to figure out what they wanted to do as both individuals and as a group. Wow! I knew you were a good mediator, but that's downright leadership."

Bob had always respected Jessica's business savvy, and her compliments were more meaningful because of it. "You know, Jessica, I've always wondered why everybody you interact with loves you. It doesn't matter who — clients, girl scout mothers, our tax guy, whoever. They always walk away from meeting you with a smile on their faces. Have you noticed that? Rarely is there a person you meet that doesn't love you."

"Well, I like it when people like me," Jess replied. "It's important for me to know I'm important to them."

"On this trip, I figured out how you do it — how you get everyone to love you. You simply seek out shared vision in every relationship you face. In a new relationship, you tactfully try to learn the needs and values of the other person. In an established relationship, you brush up on how their needs and values are coming along. Then you freely and confidently share your values. Together, it's easy for the two of you to establish some expectations of a shared outcome. Shared vision. You never turn it off, whether you're interacting with a long-time client or the bagger at the supermarket. You're always interested in where other people are coming from so that you can make an impact with them on some shared interest."

"I certainly hadn't thought of it like that," Jess was

astounded. "You're right, though. That's it. I *do* do that! To me, the most important thing in life is to make a positive impact on others. I can't do that without knowing them as fully as possible."

Bob added, "I'd like to share with you the Self-Discovery Process™. Then let's do some of the exercises that Charlotte O'Connell had us do, and uncover our true values. After that, we can do the six boxes of shared vision together. If I can have a shared vision with Chip Tronix, I certainly can have one with you ... and our family. Up to this point in our marriage, our direction has been more or less implied. I guess we've been fortunate to respect each other enough that, even when our values conflicted, we worked it out. Now we can use shared vision to aid our understanding and learn how to better support each other."

"OK, let's give it a try," Jessica said, smiling. "But I still want to see how you fit in with Chip Tronix. After that, I'll gladly do some of your exercises."

The mini-van took the exit leading home. Bob lowered his sun visor to shield his eyes from the setting sun. He was anxious to get started on his own mission. An evening and weekend with his family was the first step. It was what he needed.

He also looked forward to Monday morning, to get "his people" together and begin the deliberate process of filling in all their boxes. To match their values with company values and direction. To create a shared vision. He needed it. Chip Tronix needed it. It was that simple.

PART

HOW TO
GET STARTED

CHAPTER 12

Your Half of the
Contract for Shared Vision
Process

T HIS CHAPTER WILL HELP YOU UNDERSTAND YOUR PERSONAL
direction, regardless of what you do for a living. The
process is fairly simple, but will only yield useful
results if you take the time to consider all aspects of your life.
Arriving at your "true" personality type is very difficult when
done on your own. In this section, we'll only use one of the
four models mentioned in the story — the temperament model.
The warnings in the story about selecting the temperament
you want to be, instead of your "true" temperament, are quite
valid. Finding your temperament by yourself may be a limited
approach without using other models, including the Myers-
Briggs Type Indicator®. Unfortunately, we can't administer the
other models here (see Resources in the Appendix for a list of
administrators of the other models). To get a more objective view

of yourself, read your findings from the upcoming exercises to close friends or family and seek their feedback. Others can easily see if we're confounding ourselves with inaccurate conclusions. They often can provide a more realistic picture of how we really act and who we really are.

People sometimes ask who they can trust to give them accurate feedback. The answer of course is "everyone" and "no one." Your friends and family give you feedback from *their* perspective. What they see and how they express it runs through the lens associated with their core needs and values (their temperament). You may not know which temperament perspective they represent. For instance, feedback from a person of the Idealist temperament will be slightly different than conclusions reached by an Artisan. But you won't know which temperament a person represents unless that person has been through self-discovery and shared the results. Therefore, you'll need to seek feedback from not one but many in your trusted inner circle to ensure a complete look.

Friends and family are generally honored that you trust them enough to ask them for their thoughts. When people shy away, however, they generally have opinions they don't want to share. It's often best to leave well enough alone in that situation. Look elsewhere for your feedback. If you do pursue feedback from that person, be brave and don't shoot the messenger! They're taking a risk by sharing, so honor their honesty.

Use all of the feedback a friend or family member gives you to validate the answers you've given in the exercises that follow these instructions. Next, explain the temperaments to your confidants, and ask them to validate the temperament you've selected. If you were previously torn between two temperaments, the feedback you receive may provide more clarity on your "true" temperament.

Ready? Now follow the steps provided and complete the exercises.

Step 1: Complete the Five Year Exercise.

Instructions: Answer the three questions on the following page. For question number 1 (What five things do you want to accomplish in the next five years?), please avoid negative or destructive statements such as "I would completely destroy my competition" or "I would get rid of my house payment." Use creative statements like "I will build a house" or "I will be a podiatrist."

Five Year Exercise

List five things you will accomplish during the next five years:

What

- _____
- _____
- _____
- _____
- _____

List five things you want from your company during the next five years:

- _____
- _____
- _____
- _____
- _____

List five things your company will need to do to prosper/ survive during the next five years:

- _____
- _____
- _____
- _____
- _____

128

Step 2: Complete the Why I Work/ Why I Left Exercise.

Instructions: Take several minutes to write down why you work in your current job. If you don't formally work, list the reasons why you belong to the groups you are in. After listing all the reasons, rank their importance to you, with number one being the most important. Next, on the right side of the page list the reasons why you've left a job or group. If you haven't left a job or group, list the reasons why you would leave if provoked.

What Why I Work	Why I Left
• _____	• _____
• _____	• _____
• _____	• _____
• _____	• _____
• _____	• _____
• _____	• _____
• _____	• _____
• _____	• _____
• _____	• _____

Step 3: Complete the Typical Day Exercise & Identify Your Most Valuable Relationships.

Instructions: On the lines provided below, write down all the people you come in contact with on a typical day. For instance, "I wake up and I kiss my husband." In this case, write down your husband's name on the first line. Do that for an entire day. List the names of all the persons you see or speak to, even on the phone or via email. You'll have quite a list. Since most people use a weekday to typify their average day, you will want to also consider listing the people you only see on the weekend (e.g., at athletic events, social events, or church/synagogue). Simply add their names on the remaining lines.

Typical Day Exercise

_____

_____

_____

_____

_____

_____

_____

_____

_____

Instructions: Use the box below to identify your most valued relationships. From the list of relationships you noted on the previous page, which persons currently provide you with (or you wish provided you) the inspiration, personal growth, value and need fulfillment you mentioned in the Five Year Exercise?

Identify Your Relationships	
Work	**Family**
Friends	**Other**

Who

Step 4: Identify Your Core Needs and Values.

You might have seen yourself in some of the patterns listed in the story and have an inclination as to which temperament is the best fit for you. The characters represented typical needs and values of the four temperaments (see matrix on following page).

In the next several pages you'll see how you exercise the values and seek to satisfy the needs represented in all four of the temperaments. Your quest here is to discover the one temperament that best fits your core needs. Your core psychological needs must be met in the activities you undertake daily, otherwise you'll seek out other things to do. This is a critical point when considering your job.

Identify Your Core Needs and Values	
IDEALIST Lloyd	**GUARDIAN** Bob
RATIONAL Sharon Ramin	**ARTISAN** Jessica Terry

Most likely, you will not be able to accurately determine your core needs in this section. One reason has to do with the maturing process. As you progress through life, you begin to recognize the importance of values other than your own, at which point you more actively include those values in your life. This experimentation, while important in personal growth and maturity, confuses us as to who we really are. For all our good intentions, satisfying those other needs and values still leaves us short in the quest for satisfying those of our own temperament.

Other reasons for inaccuracy include overbearing environmental pressures (e.g., excessive performance expectations on the job, in school, or even from authority figures such as parents). Of course, undue stress regardless of source may require behaviors that obscure our ability to see our "true" temperament.

Even in stress-free environments, most of us strive to achieve values we previously had no interest in or found tragically lacking in our lives. This strong compulsion can also make identifying "true" personality type and temperament illusive. For a complete understanding of your "true" type, see the recommended resource list in the appendix.

Instructions: Review each of the temperament description pages that follow. As you read the narratives and review the lists, circle words or phrases that capture you. If you identified with a character from the story, validate the needs and values that he or she represented on the appropriate temperament page.

At the bottom of each temperament page, use the spaces provided to identify how you exercise the needs and values of that temperament in your life. The purpose is not to identify a single temperament yet, but rather to recognize how values from each temperament are present in your life. If you have only a few examples, that's OK. Simply move on to the next page.

Artisan Temperament

The Artisan core needs are *to have the freedom to act without hindrance and to see a marked result from action*. They highly value aesthetics, whether in nature or art. Their energies are focused on skillful performance, variety and stimulation. They tend toward pragmatic, utilitarian actions with a focus on technique. They trust their impulses and have a drive to action. The Artisan's learning style is often concrete, random and experiential. Artisans enjoy hands-on, applied learning with a fast pace and freedom to explore.

What I need from others: I need others to give me space. I enjoy people, but I find too many expectations confining. I want to be appreciated for my troubleshooting talents by being relieved of constraints on my freedom when there is no crisis.

How others perceive me: Other people see me as fun, quick and risk-taking. They believe things come to me easily and that I am lucky. They often see me as a maverick or free spirit. They think I am a lot of fun to be around, but they want me to prove I am reliable.

THE ARTISAN		
	Communication Style:	Colorful
	Communicates with:	Anecdotes and Questions
	At Work, Promotes:	Opportunity
	Workplace Strengths:	Producing and Performing
	Best Environment:	Stimulating and Varied

Adapted with permission from Linda V. Berens, *Understanding Yourself and Others, An Introduction to Temperament* (Telos Publications, CA, 1998).

My Artisan needs and values:

_____

_____

_____

_____

_____

_____

Where in my life I satisfy them:

_____

_____

_____

_____

_____

_____

Guardian Temperament

The Guardian core needs are for *group membership and responsibility.* They need to know they are doing the responsible thing. They value stability, security and a sense of community. They trust hierarchy and authority, and may be surprised when others go against these social structures. Guardians perfer cooperative actions with a focus on standards and norms. Their orientation is to their past experiences and they like things sequenced and structured. Guardians tend to look for the practical applications of what they are learning.

What I need from others: I need to be appreciated for the simple way I support others day to day. A sincere 'thank you' or a special gesture that will make things easier for me go a long way. I like to be asked to be included in projects and events even though I may not always have time to participate. When people follow through on commitments and fulfill their responsibilities in a timely manner, it is more than a courtesy; it demonstrates their respect for me.

How others perceive me: Other people see me as organized, courteous, responsible and loyal. They know I am someone they can count on to help out in whatever way I can. Sometimes people think I am too structured and organized, and not spontaneous enough. People generally describe me as a good student, spouse, parent, friend or co-worker.

THE GUARDIAN

Communication Style:	Factual
Communicates with:	Comparatives and Measurement
At Work, Promotes:	Structure
Workplace Strengths:	Administering and Servicing
Best Environment:	Organized and Secure

Adapted with permission from Linda V. Berens, *Understanding Yourself and Others, An Introduction to Temperament* (Telos Publications, CA, 1998).

My Guardian needs and values:

_____

_____

_____

_____

_____

Where in my life I satisfy them:

_____

_____

_____

_____

_____

Rational Temperament

The Rational core needs are for *mastery of concepts, knowledge and competence.* They want to understand the operating principles of the universe and learn or even develop theories for everything. They value expertise, logical consistency, concepts and ideas, and seek progress. Rationals tend toward pragmatic, utilitarian actions with a technology focus. Rationals trust logic above all else. They tend to be skeptical and highly value precision in language. Their learning style is conceptual. Rationals want to know the underlying principles that generate the details and facts rather than the details alone.

What I need from others: Allow me to think for myself and give me room to be creative. I want to be taken seriously. Don't rush me if you want quality. Work with me to meet long-term goals even if they don't seem to have immediate payoff.

How others perceive me: Generally I am perceived as intelligent. They may also view me as lacking emotion, or they misinterpret what emotion I do show. They often view me as having particular talents rather than seeing my talents as intrinsic to who I am.

THE RATIONAL		
Communication Style:	Scholarly
Communicates with:	Conditionals and Precise Definitions
At Work, Promotes:	Efficiency
Workplace Strengths:	Designing and Planning
Best Environment:	Innovative and Intellectual

Adapted with permission from Linda V. Berens, *Understanding Yourself and Others, An Introduction to Temperament* (Telos Publications, CA, 1998).

My Rational needs and values:

_____

_____

_____

_____

_____

_____

Where in my life I satisfy them:

_____

_____

_____

_____

_____

_____

Idealist Temperament

The Idealist core needs are for the *meaning and significance that come from having a sense of purpose and working toward some greater good.* They need to have a sense of unique identity. They value unity, self-actualization and authenticity. Idealists prefer co-operative interactions with a focus on ethics and morality. They tend to trust their intuitions and impressions first, then seek to find the logic and the data to support them. Given their need for empathic relationships, they learn more easily when they can relate to the instructor or the group.

What I need from others: A personal connection is imperative for me. I must feel the other person is acting authentically and will accept me if I act authentically. I expect open discourse and personal sharing. I want to tell my stories as well as listen to theirs. I need some feedback that they believe in me and my life purpose.

How others perceive me: Other people view me as a people person, someone who demonstrates empathy easily and makes others feel good about who they are. They commend my communication skills and say I am a natural teacher, counselor and mentor. They may describe me as imaginative, idealistic, mysterious, intuitive, gullible, friendly, empowering, committed and genuine.

THE IDEALIST		
	Communication Style:	Dramatic
	Communicates with:	Metaphors and Universals
	At Work, Promotes:	Growth
	Workplace Strengths:	Promoting and Training
	Best Environment:	Expressive and Personal

Adapted with permission from Linda V. Berens, *Understanding Yourself and Others, An Introduction to Temperament* (Telos Publications, CA, 1998).

My Idealist needs and values:	Where in my life I satisfy them:
_____	_____
_____	_____
_____	_____
_____	_____
_____	_____

Instructions: At this point, you may know which temperament houses your core needs and values. Generally, participants can see the reality of the core needs when they fill in real life examples. If, however, you have difficulty selecting a primary temperament, use the opposite approach. Which one is least like you? Cross that temperament out. Of the remainder, which one could you do without? Cross that one out. This approach should narrow your search down to only two possible temperaments. Of these two, which core needs could you not live without? What do you hold onto the tightest?

If you still are unable to distinguish, call someone on the resource list in the appendix for help!

My Best Fit Temperament	
IDEALIST	GUARDIAN
RATIONAL	ARTISAN

Step 5: Defining Your Values.

Our values guide us in meeting our core psychological needs. We use them to decide whether or not to enter a relationship or job. It follows, then, that we leave relationships or jobs when those values are not present.

Instructions: Go to page 129 and the "Why I Left" exercise. Examine each position you've left and determine: (1) which values were missing at the time? (2) which values from your "Best Fit" Temperament, below, were missing?

Defining Your Values	
IDEALIST VALUES	**GUARDIAN VALUES**
Empathic relationships, unity, cooperative interaction, self-actualization, idealized and meaningful world, authenticity, ethics and morality.	Group/bonding relationships, stability, hierarchical procedures, security, preservation of social groups, conformity, rules and regulations.
RATIONAL VALUES	**ARTISAN VALUES**
Expert relationships, logical consistency, scientific inquiry, intelligence, ultimate truths or theories, progress, concepts and ideas.	Fraternal relationships, variety, performance with skill, action, immediate adventure, aesthetics, excitement and stimulation.

**Write down your "must have" values
on the following page.**

My Values

How

In order for me to perform my duties/job and not leave the company, these values must be present:

_____

_____

_____

_____

_____

_____

_____

_____

_____

Step 6: Defining Your Mission.

You currently are meeting the core values and needs of your temperament in your life. The question is: where in your life are they satisfied? When they are satisfied in a well-rounded manner at both work and at home, people are happy and fulfilled. When they are fulfilled only at work, personal problems may eventually overtake the individual (marital problems, child behavior problems, burnout, etc.), and the individual either becomes unproductive or leaves the company. When core needs and values are met only at home, the individual is generally minimally productive at work and will eventually leave the organization for a more fulfilling job — seeking that elusive "opportunity for advancement."

We are now going to address the balance of your core values and needs by bringing them together in the *who, what,* and *how* of your life.

Instructions Part 1: Go to the "Who" box on page 131. In the "Identify Your Relationships" section, circle relationships that currently help you fulfill your core needs and values. Now rank your relationships in order of importance with the numbers 1, 2, and 3.

Instructions Part 2: Go to the "What" boxes on pages 128 and 129. In section one of the "Five Year Exercise" and in the "Why I Work" exercise, circle items which currently fulfill your core needs. You may find some needs are not fulfilled in your answers. In that case, make a note of the missing need and put a square around it. Now rank your items in order of importance with the numbers 4, 5, and 6.

Instructions Part 3: Go to the "How" box on page 140. Circle your top three values from the "My Values" exercise. You may find some important values are not represented in your answers. Once again, make a note of the missing value and put a square around it. Rank your values in order of importance with the numbers 7, 8, and 9.

My "Mission"

My Relationships

(From Page 131)

(1) _____

(2) _____

(3) _____

I Need to Have

What

(From Page 128 & 129)

My Values

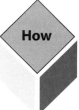

(From Page 140)

(4) _____   (7) _____

(5) _____   (8) _____

(6) _____   (9) _____

Instructions Part 4: Insert your answers 1 through 9 in the spaces provided below.

I recognize these values as guiding my life:
(7)_____, (8)_____, and
(9)_____. I will accomplish
(4)_____, (5)_____,
and (6)_____, so as
to support and grow my relationships with
(1)_____, (2)_____, and
(3)_____.

Step 7: Examining Your Mission Statement.

Take a look at your mission statement above. Are the relationships, values, and needs you've listed mostly centered around your work life or home life? You should have a sampling from both in each of the three areas. If not, you run the risks mentioned in Step 6.

You may have noted where you'd like to make changes in the values and needs you choose to fulfill while doing the exercises. These notes showed up as squares in your answers. If you have a large number of squares, you may have been using a lot of adaptive behavior at work and in your relationships. Don't be overly aggressive in seeking to now satisfy those core needs. Simply knowing what to look for will aid your decision-making in the future.

Summary.

Congratulations! You just completed the first half of the

Contract for Shared Vision

process. At this point, many people wish to set up goals to support their personal mission statement. Please feel free to do so.

In our effort to arrive at a shared vision, however, we are only half way done. The second half of our process concerns the core values and needs of the group. This book doesn't lend itself to such an endeavor, although many people creatively complete the process on their own. Some buy many copies of this book, have everyone complete it, then bring them together for the group session. Others copy Bob's idea of writing down the answers to the six boxes on pieces of paper. In either case, you can use the contract that Sharon wrote up to bring your group to shared vision.

After you have your contract in hand, the question of direction is solved. From that point it's a simple process of conducting short- and long-term goal setting to commit to the agreement. Once again, facilitators exist to help you in this process and are listed in the appendix.

Shared vision helps a "system" of people interact and agree on what needs to be done. It doesn't matter if the system is a single person or a group of people. Shared vision allows collaboration between any two systems. Just as technology aids us in task fulfillment, understanding and using temperament to secure the common goals of shared vision enables our personal fulfillment. Enjoy.

Bibliography and Recommended Reading

Belasco, J. and Stayer, R. *Flight of the Buffalo*. New York: Warner Books, 1993.

Berens, L. *Understanding Yourself and Others: An Introduction to Temperament*. Huntington Beach, CA: Telos Publications, 1998.

Berens, L. and Nardi, D. *The 16 Personality Types: Descriptions for Self-Discovery*. Huntington Beach, CA: Telos Publications, 1999.

Beyham, W. and Cox, J. *Zapp: The Lightning of Empowerment*. New York: Fawcett Columbine, 1988.

Blanchard, K., Carew, D. and Parsisi-Carew, E. *The One Minute Manager Builds High Performance Teams*. New York: William Morrow and Company, Inc., 1990.

Brandenburger, A. and Nalebuff, B. *Co-opetition*. New York: Doubleday, 1996.

Bridges, W. *The Character of Organizations*. Palo Alto, CA: Davies-Black Publishing, 1992.

Covey, S. *The 7 Habits of Highly Effective People*. New York: Simon & Schuster, 1990.

Fisher, D. *The Simplified Baldridge Award Organization Assessment.* New York: Lincoln-Bradley Publishing Group, 1993.

Hammer, M. and Champy, J. *Reengineering the Corporation.* New York: Harper Business, 1993.

Handy, C. *The Age of Unreason.* Boston, MA: Harvard Business School Press, 1990.

Heifetz, R. *Leadership Without Easy Answers.* Cambridge, MA: Belknap Press (Harvard), 1994.

Hersey, P., Blanchard, K. and Johnson, D. *Management of Organizational Behavior (Seventh Edition).* Upper Saddle River, NJ: Prentice Hall, 1996.

Isachsen, O. and Berens, L. *Working Together: A Personality-Centered Approach to Management.* San Juan Capistrano, CA: Institute for Management Development, 1988.

Keirsey, D. *Please Understand Me II.* Distributed by: Prometheus Nemisis Book Company, Del Mar, California, 1998.

Kohn, A. *Punished by Rewards: The Trouble With Gold Stars, Incentive Plans, Praise and Other Bribes.* Boston: Houghton Mifflin Company, 1993.

Nardi, D. *Character and Personality Type: Discovering Your Uniqueness for Career and Relationship Success.* Huntington Beach, CA: Telos Publications, 1999.

Senge, P. *The Fifth Discipline.* New York: Currency Doubleday, 1990.

Tieger, P. and Barron-Tieger, B. *Do What You Are.* Boston: Little, Brown and Company, 1995.

Walton, M. *The Deming Management Method.* New York: Perigee Books, 1996.

Wright, L. *Twins And What They Tell Us About Who We Are.* New York: John Wiley & Sons, Inc., 1997.

About the Author

David Specht is the CEO of Triumphant Leadership Solutions, Inc., in Colorado Springs, Colorado. He has more than 15 years of experience in consulting and training across the United States.

Mr. Specht is a former Director of the Leadership Department, United States Officer Training School, Lackland AFB, Texas. This assignment began a five-year study of all aspects of leadership theory and application. Since that time, he's trained thousands of business leaders and Air Force officers in the areas of Leadership, Total Quality Management, and Team Building.

A 1983 graduate of the United States Air Force Academy, Mr. Specht has served in many leadership positions in both fighter and trainer jet aircraft flying units.

Resources

For facilitation of the **Contract for Shared Vision** process or the Self-Discovery Process™:

Triumphant Leadership Solutions, Inc.
www.tlsteams.com
800-364-4240

For facilitation of the Self-Discovery Process[SM], training to become certified to be able to facilitate the Self-Discovery Process™ or assistance in clarifying *best-fit personality type:*

Temperament Research Institute
www.tri-network.com
800-700-4874

Notes

Notes

Notes

Notes

Notes

Order Form

Fax Orders:	714.841.0312
Telephone Orders:	Call Toll Free: 1.800.700.4874
	Please have your AMEX, VISA,
	or MasterCard ready.
Online Orders:	http://www.telospublications.com
Postal Orders:	Telos Publications
	P.O. Box 4457
	Huntington Beach, CA 92605-4457
	Tel: 714.841.0041
Sales Tax:	Please add 7.75% for books
	shipped to California addresses.
Shipping Information:	$4.00 for the first book and
	$1.50 for each additional book
Payment Information:	☐ Check
	☐ VISA ☐ MasterCard ☐ AMEX

Card Number: _____

Name on Card: _____

Expiration Date: _____

No. of Copies @ $14.95 ea: _____

Sales Tax (CA Residents): _____

Shipping: _____

Total: _____

**CALL TOLL FREE
AND ORDER NOW**

Company Name: _____

Name: _____

Address: _____

City: _____ **State:** _____ **Zip:** _____

Telephone: (_____) _____